To Clare,

Your future will be bright and this living hope within will never disappoint you.

Proverbs 24:14 TPT.

Blessings and love,

Jenny Watson.

DETERMINE YOUR *Direction*

A DEVOTIONAL JOURNEY

Activating you into a successful future

JENNY WATSON

DETERMINE YOUR DIRECTION
Copyright © 2022 Jenny Watson
Paperback ISBN: 13.9798821191427

All rights reserved. No part of this publication may be reproduced, stored in a retrieval system, or transmitted in any form or by any means, electronic, mechanical, photocopying or otherwise, without prior written consent of the publisher except as provided by under United Kingdom copyright law. Short extracts may be used for review purposes with credits given.

Unless otherwise stated, all Scripture contained within this book is taken from the New King James Version®. (NKJV®) Copyright © 1982 by Thomas Nelson. Used by permission. All rights reserved.

Scripture taken from the Amplified Bible Classic Edition®. (AMPC®) Copyright © 1954, 1958, 1962, 1964, 1965, 1987 by the Lockman Foundation. Used by permission. All rights reserved. (www.lockman.org)

Scripture taken from the New American Standard Bible®. (NASB®) Copyright © 1960, 1971, 1977, 1995, 2020 by the Lockman Foundation. Used by permission. All rights reserved. (www.lockman.org)

Scripture taken from the King James Version®. (KJV®) Rights in the Authorised (King James) Version os the Bible are vested in the Crown. Used by permission. All rights reserved.

Scripture taken from The Passion Translation®. (TPT®) Copyright © 2020 Passion & Fire Ministries, Inc.® Used by permission. All rights reserved.

Scripture taken from the English Standard Version®. (ESV®) Copyright © 2001 by Crossway, a publishing ministry of Good News Publishers. Used by permission. All rights reserved.

Scripture taken from the New Living Translation®. (NLT®) Copyright © 1996, 2004, 2007, 2015 by Tyndale House Foundation. Used by permission. All rights reserved.

Scripture taken from the Tree of Life Version®. (TLV®) Copyright © 2014, 2016 by the Tree of Life Bible Society. Used by permission of the Tree of Life Bible Society. All rights reserved.

Scripture taken from the the Holy Bible, New International Version®. (NIV®) Copyright © 1973, 1978, 1984, 2011 by Biblica, Inc.® Used by permission of Zondervan. All rights reserved worldwide.

Edited by:
Tracey Taylor Freelance Editor
(KVC & Hummingbird Coaching)
office@tracetaylor.co.uk

Cover design and illustrations by:
Lamplight Art Michaela
 (lamplight.art@gmail.com)

Published by:
Jane Gibbs KDP Publishing Services
jgibbscreative@btinternet.com

Contents

Dedication	11
Acknowledgements	13
Endorsements	15
Foreword	21
Introduction	25
Day 1. Enjoy the Journey	31
Day 2. Overcoming Obstacles	39
Day 3. Attitude	51
Day 4. Believe for Breakthrough	57
Day 5. Choose Your Company	63
Day 6. What Delights You?	69
Day 7. *Selah Reflection: Understanding Shabbat Rest*	73
Day 8. Encounters	77
Day 9. Forgiveness	83
Day 10. Grow Up and You Will Go Up	89
Day 11. Hurry	93
Day 12. Instruction	97
Day 13. Joy	105
Day 14. *Selah Reflection: Understanding Shabbat Rest*	111
Day 15. Contagious Kindness	113
Day 16. Live, Love, Laugh	119
Day 17. Momentum	129

Day 18. Nourished to Flourish	137
Day 19. Seize Every Opportunity	141
Day 20. Pause, Pray, Purpose	147
Day 21. **Selah Reflection: Understanding Shabbat Rest**	151
Day 22. Question Time	155
Day 23. Reach Out for Revelation	159
Day 24. Strategy	165
Day 25. Thankfulness	169
Day 26. Unique	175
Day 27. Vision in the Valleys	179
Day 28. **Selah Reflection: Understanding Shabbat Rest**	183
Day 29. Wise Words Win	187
Day 30. Extend, Expand, Enlarge	193
Day 31. Yes & Amen	197
Day 32. Zeal	201
Day 33. Remain Flexible	207
Day 34. Continuing the Journey with Proverbs: Watch where you are going!	211
Day 35. **Selah Reflection: Understanding Shabbat Rest**	215
Footnotes	219

Dedication

The reason I live is to worship Jesus and I owe all that I am to Him alone.

I dedicate this book in gratitude to the most wonderful husband and soulmate with whom I have the joy of sharing life. The adventures together only get better - thank you for being my greatest supporter and for keeping things in perspective for me. I also owe a debt of gratitude to wonderful parents, my mum now in heaven and my dad sharing our home with us. Thank you for being a great example of a disciplined life. Thank you for providing a stable and secure home, which made it easy for me to believe in a good good heavenly Father.

Acknowledgements

My best friend, Maria, has taught me the true meaning of Jesus words, *"No one has greater love [nor stronger commitment] than to lay down his own life for his friends." - John 15:13, (AMPC)*. We have worked through the full scope of emotions - the joys and sorrows and the highs and lows of life many times - and we live to tell the story. You are a true friend and a trophy of his grace. Thank you for walking alongside me. You spurred me on to write this. May I be a true friend to you as you have been to me.

I am grateful to the new friends that the Lord has brought across my path in this process too. Thank you, Julie Brown, for your help in the publishing process and encouragement to go for it. My gratitude to Tracey Taylor for your inspiration and willingness to edit the manuscript. To Michaela Langford for creating such masterpieces in art from my musings.

And my dear friend Rachel Hickson who has helped me navigate through choppy waters and always loved and believed in me. You are an amazing example and mentor to many, I am privileged to call you friend. Thank you for writing the foreword in this, my first book.

Determine Your Direction

I have been privileged to be mentored by dynamic and formidable women, though miles away, you are close in heart: To Carole Pearce who helped shape me and gave me a true example to follow of surrender and whole hearted devotion to God and Anne Tate who imparted confidence and pulled me forward when I couldn't see a way through. I salute and honour these precious ones who make a way for others to grow.

Endorsements

Jenny Watson has done a great job in presenting the Body of Christ with a brand-new devotional in a non-traditional way.

I loved the way it is written to be digested in 35 days. Many times, I lose my way in a year-long devotional! However, I will return to this one over and over again in order to renew and increase focus in order to keep moving in the right direction. In my experience, I have met many believers who do not know what their call, destiny or direction is. It is also key to know that sometimes with the advent of a new season or a new era like we are in now, we are required to move in a new direction to accomplish what is on the Lord's heart. As we mature in the Lord our direction changes or what we are called to bring forth for the Lord.

This book will be valuable to new believers that are learning to move in intimacy with the Lord and stay in daily relationship with Holy Spirit. In addition, Determining Your Direction will be powerful to establish mature believers that are wanting more of Him and less of them. Jenny has expressed clearly, simply and powerfully what the Lord is speaking to us right now in order to release His voice and stand in His character.

Determine Your Direction

I believe this book to be a beginning of a series of devotionals on the various aspects of functioning in Kingdom and delivering harvest.

Anne S Tate,
International Director of Prayer and the Watches,
Glory of Zion, International, Apostolic Watchman

This may seem an unusual way to start an endorsement, but Jenny is one of the easiest people I have found to be a friend with. She exudes joy and I am attracted to joyful people. Another quality about her is humility, what you see is what you get, a woman very much after God's own heart.

There are a lot of devotionals available in bookshops and online. However, if you want authenticity through the lens of someone's life experiences, then you can certainly identify with Jenny's, which brings home the truth of God's word lived out through everyday life. I commend this devotional to anyone searching for more of God in a focused and authentic way. It is written by a woman who has and still is walking the walk. There could not be a better devotional for now if you truly are a God seeker. I encourage you to enjoy the journey as you set your compass to determine the right direction for the next season of your life.

David Adeola -The Gatekeeper ®

Endorsements

In Determine Your Direction Jenny Watson takes the reader on a journey to freedom, focus and fulfilment. Each day you will be inspired by Jenny's personal stories as well as the challenge to incorporate godly principles into your spiritually healthy lifestyle. As you read prepare to experience the spirit of breakthrough as you move towards your highest call.

Jane Hamon
Vision Church @ Christian International,
Author: Dreams & Visions, The Deborah Company,
Discernment, Declarations for Breakthrough

I have known Jenny for a number of years and whenever people ask me about her, I invariably comment that of her many qualities the one that stands out for me is her devotion to Jesus. It therefore comes as no surprise that her first book is a devotional. In Determine your Direction Jenny gives us daily nuggets that will strengthen, encourage, stretch and provoke us in our journey to know the Lord. With great wisdom she has created time to pause so truth can be absorbed and applied. I truly believe this will become an invaluable resource to thousands of people in their daily walk with Jesus. I wholeheartedly endorse this book knowing your life will be changed as you read and apply the truths contained in its pages

Mark Curtis - Passion for Jesus Ministries UK

Determine Your Direction

When a prophet writes a devotional it becomes in its essence a key for the way ahead. Holy Spirit has used our friend Jenny Watson to put these topics together not just to encourage, but to equip and strengthen the readers as they grow into their divine assignment. It is a preparation to access divine destiny in these challenging times, written out of years of experience and relationship with Holy Spirit. We highly recommend this Devotional as a part of your tool kit for the days ahead.

Gerhard Bals and Eulalee King Bals
International House of Apostolic Reformation
Iserlohn Germany

With many Daily Devotionals available, Jenny has brought a fresh perspective on taking in spiritual nourishment whilst moving forward. Determine Your Direction will enable you to stay focused on the horizon whilst developing a deeper daily walk with the Lord. Jenny shares foundational truths and nuggets from her own journey in this invitation to discover the greater things God has for you.

Jennifer LeClaire
Senior leader of the Awakening House of Prayer global movement

Determine Your Direction is an awesome book by Jenny Watson. This devotional journey is meant to activate you into a successful future. One of the most important things to understand in our lives, especially during changing times, is the direction that God has for us. The chapter

I love most is Live, Love and Laugh. Only through joy do we have the strength to accomplish the directives we were created to accomplish.

We also want to better know how to embrace our "Process of Time", which is an important Biblical concept. The season of life that you are going through is linking you to a heavenly order that the Creator has destined for you. However, if you don't process a season correctly, you don't have clear perspective of who you are and what you are about.

God's perfect timing occurs when Heaven's gates and earth gates align and connect, and you are standing ready to move into the next dimension of your life. You enter by faith. When we position ourselves to be at the right place at the right time, we hear God, grab hold of His covenant best, and step into the next phase our destiny.

Faith comes by hearing, and hearing by the word that God is speaking to us now, in time. Even in our daily Scripture reading, we need to remember that we are communing from a place and time today, and not just attempting to understand faith that occurred in history. From faith today, we express action that produces change. God's words were recorded for us in the past, but how He is speaking them today is what quickens us to evaluate and understand the world from His perspective. We are actually watching events in Scripture unfold prophetically in our present time and analysing our circumstances from the revelation and illumination being imparted today, from yesterday and into tomorrow.

Get ready! Determine Your Direction will help you gain momentum on the path that you were created to walk forward on.

Dr. Chuck D. Pierce

President of Glory of Zion International,

Kingdom Harvest Alliance, and Global Spheres Inc.

Foreword

It is my delight to be able to write this foreword for my friend, Jenny Watson, for her first book, *Determine Your Direction*. This personal, yet challenging, devotional gives you stepping stones to help you navigate life well. Too often, we let life happen to us rather than taking the intentional footsteps to determine our future direction. This book encourages you to be bold and make those deliberate choices and then watch how different your life can be.

Recently I was reflecting on Jesus and how Hebrews describes Him, *"Jesus Christ is the same yesterday and today and forever."* (Hebrews 13:8 NIV). I realised that to live a life like Jesus' I, too, needed to have a perspective that is able to balance my past, my present and future, in a healthy way. Too often, our guilt and even our over-anxious feelings of integrity, can make us live life with a sense of constant apology and insecurity. The lens of our self-worth and direction is only through our past… We limit our forward momentum and achievements of tomorrow, with the constant narrative of yesterday. We do need to look back, find the truth and forgiveness, but then learn the art of forward direction. In this book, Jenny carefully shares stories and life experiences, packed with practical tools, to help you achieve this directive. As Jenny outlines in her words, often we carry words for years, waiting for that perfect epiphany moment that never seems to come. But *today* is the time to make those determined decisions which alter the course of your life. Living courageously and conscientiously in your *today*, will determine your future destination.

As you let the stories and the Word of God in this book penetrate your soul, let it stir again the wild imaginations of all you can achieve in your tomorrow. Choose not to be someone who says "I have learnt not to dream too much as I only get disappointed," electing to live a limited, cautious life with no risky expectations because of the pain of yesterday. You have been made to carry a passionate, enthusiastic hope for your future.

This book will refocus your thinking and reset some of your rhythms in life. I would encourage you to make the most of the "Selah" moments at the end of each week. This word, Selah, literally encourages us to stop, step back, consider, realign our life and thinking and then re-engage and move forward. Also find a friend to walk this journey with. Two are always better than one - you have so much more fun!! This book, *Determine Your Direction*, needs you to start a journey of honesty and transparency with Jesus and your own soul. In our lives today we are so often product orientated rather than process observant. We just want to drive through and collect our order; we do not want to be bothered with the logistics of the process to produce the result. But our

Foreword

God is a God of stories and journeys. There are no shortcuts and often there even seem to be laborious detours. But as you decide to be resolute about your life's path, God will answer your heart's cry and direct your life. This is your season of satisfaction!

Rachel Hickson

Director/Founder Heartcry for Change

www.Heartcryforchange.com

March, 2022

Introduction

"There are two roads in this life and if you are on the wrong one, you need to think carefully and change your ways." This was one of the last conversations to take place between a mother and her eldest son before she passed away six months later. She was of course right, trying desperately to reach his heart to encourage him to change his ways, but alas to each is given the choice as to what we do in this wonderful journey called life.

In 2021, I heard the still small voice of the Lord speak, directing me to release a daily devotional type word on social media for a thirty-day period. It was an assignment which demanded discipline every day until its completion. Firstly, I had to overcome limiting beliefs, time restraints and other hurdles (some of my own making) to do this. However, I was determined to complete and I did! It taught me a great deal. I had expectations and hopes and now looking back, I see that some were realised whilst others were not met. But through it all I learned, I changed, I accomplished and I gained much from taking this step of obedience.

One Thing Leads to Another

The book that you hold in your hand is a fulfilment of dreams and vision but also of prophetic words that have been spoken over my life over many years. I now wonder if this would ever of happened if I hadn't have taken that small step of producing the thirty day release on social media. In the midst of that process, the opportunity came for me to discover all that I needed to know about how to go forward in writing, publishing and releasing my own book. When opportunities come our way, it behoves us to recognise and seize them. This whole process has not been without its challenges and setbacks, but through it all I have learned great lessons, discovered new terrain and developed immensely.

This ***Determine Your Direction*** devotional is intended to give a focus to your immediate future, by presenting a nugget of truth each day for you to think about and hopefully, for you to apply to your life.

The focus each day includes the dynamic and powerful Word of God which is able to transform anyone and anything. It is able to align everything to the purpose and will of our Creator and good, good Father.

For the word of God is living and active and sharper than any two

edged sword-piercing right through to a separation of soul and spirit, joints and marrow, and able to judge the thoughts and intentions of the heart.
(Hebrews 4:12 TLV)

Another Discovery

Over the last ten years, we have had the joy of discovering the life and power there is in being grafted into our Jewish root. We have explored and taught much on the "One New Man" (Ephesians 2:15) and "God's Appointed Times" (Leviticus 23:2). It is with this backdrop that I want to present this devotional in six-day sections, punctuated by one day for reflection. This is to give space to breathe, pause, and allow the Spirit of God to work His good Word deeply into your soul. You may of course choose to work through in a different rhythm, if that suits you better.

We all Need Somebody to Lean on

So, the LORD spoke to Moses face to face, as a man speaks to his friend.
(Exodus 33:11, NKJV)

A friend loves at all times, and a brother is born for adversity.
(Proverbs 17:17)

A man who has friends must himself be friendly, but there is a friend who sticks closer than a brother.
(Proverbs 18:24)

The Value of a Friend

Two are better than one, because they have a good reward for their labor. For if they fall, one will lift up his companion. But woe to him who is alone when he falls, for he has no one to help him up. Again, if two lie down together, they will keep warm; but how can one be warm alone? Though one may be overpowered by another, two can withstand him. And a threefold cord is not quickly broken.
(Ecclesiastes 4:9-13, AMPC)

Ointment and perfume delight the heart, and the sweetness of a man's friend gives delight by hearty counsel.
(Proverbs 27:9, NKJV)

As iron sharpens iron, so a man sharpens the countenance of his friend. (Proverbs 27:17)

Introduction

We need friends on our journey to walk alongside us in the valleys, to lift up our heart and cheer us on the way, and also to share the highlights, victories, and joys that come our way. True friends enable the best in us and cover our weaknesses. Some friends become mentors to us that coach our thoughts and actions in the right way. I am grateful for those I am able to call my friends and I hope through this book that I will meet and make many more. For you, my prayer is that as you journey through this devotional you will know you are not alone, it is written with you in mind and for your best. Let's embark on this venture together, each successfully reaching our destination, having accomplished all assignments for which we were designed, created, appointed and authorised. Let's not be amongst the crowd who never find their true purpose and fail to fulfil their destiny, but let's set sail, with our faces to the wind, and move forward.

Enjoy the next phase of your journey…as you ***determine your direction***!

DAY ONE

Enjoy the Journey

There is a joy in the journey,
There's a light we can love on the way.
There is a wonder and wildness to life,
And freedom for those who obey.
All those who seek it shall find it,
A pardon for all who believe.
Hope for the hopeless and sight for the blind.

To all who've been born of the Spirit
And who share incarnation with Him;
Who belong to eternity, stranded in time,
And weary of struggling with sin.
Forget not the hope that's before you,
And never stop counting the cost.
Remember the hopelessness when you were lost?

'Joy In The Journey', by Michael Card. From the album *The Final Word*.
Copyright © 1987, Whole Amor Publishing.

This song impacted me in my early formative years as a believer in Jesus. Whatever bad stuff has gone on, is going on right now or might yet be dumped in your path, there is a promise from heaven that joy and a true, deep and lasting assurance can be found, if you consider the claims and receive the gift of eternal life in Yeshua, Jesus Christ.

Life is about Relationships

We are taking a journey together. Life is about the people we grow with, meet and develop relationships with and how we encounter, influence, bless and impact one another. Yet we are bombarded by information that seems to come at us at a hurtling speed. Life is more than information and equipment. We are made to relate as one human being to another.

The Information Tsunami

We often find ourselves contending with information overload. It is difficult to process so much at once and this is often a contributing factor to stress related sickness.

According to mathematician and futurist Buckminster Fuller and his "Knowledge Doubling Curve" trajectory statement, it took 4,350 years since records began for human knowledge to double the first time, less than a quarter of that time for the second 'doubling' to occur (1,250 years), followed by a massive decrease of only 350 years for the third wave. Then, the doubling of human knowledge speeds up exponentially... The fourth wave took just twenty-four years, the fifth - five years - with a further decrease to three years by the sixth wave. By the time we arrive at 1986, the doubling reached a staggering one-and-a-half years. From that point on, it is estimated that knowledge has been doubling *every year*![1] World-wide computer manufacturer IBM predicted the likelihood of knowledge doubling every 11-12 hours by 2020.

We are a product of our decisions not a product of our circumstances. Often, we are unable to control the circumstances around us. The situations we find ourselves in may not be a result of our own actions. We may not have caused the situation as it is presented, but we can determine how we will respond to it. We do have a choice in our reaction and perspective.

I want you to consider this and see that one of the greatest weapons against negativity and against stress is our ability to choose one thought above another. We will unpack this further during our time together. Considering our daily choice is a discipline and since we are focusing on the importance of relationships in our lives, you might want to think about the individuals you could share your journey with. We need people on the journey. We need others to sharpen us. We need friends to mirror back to us, to encourage us. We need those who will lift us up and help keep us focused, with right perspective on things.

It is also good to think about our vision and the horizon that is before us. Some of you may have let go of dreams and vision. Maybe the vision is there, but it is dormant, waiting for the right spark to reignite and refuel the passion and fire necessary to light your dreams up again. All is not lost…if there is a spark of vision within you, there is the possibility of fulfilment. This book is evidence of that very thing.

If you are a living soul, then you have promises and destiny in your life yet to be fulfilled! Think about your potential for a moment… You are made in the image of the Creator of all that is in this world. He is actually limitless and that truth, right there, gives you licence to dream big! If you are deciding to commit to joining this journey for the next 35 days, pause for a moment to think about what you hope to gain and what you would like the outcome to be. There will be a review at the end and we can look at some next steps to take if you want to go further and deeper. It is the small decisions that we make daily that make up the huge strides we find we've made when we actually look back. Just keep going at it little by little and you will be able to turn around and say, "look how far I've come."

You can also ask the Lord Jesus to help you. Wherever you are in your journey with Him, it is good to be reminded that He has made you for friendship with Him and has written a good destiny over your life. So why not invite Him to be involved? Submit to Jesus the things that you are not sure about, or that you are finding difficult, or that you are struggling to process. Ask for His help over the course of these next 35 days as you *determine your direction*. He will be there to encourage you. He will want to celebrate each small step achieved with you. He wants to champion your victories and to lift your arms when you are feeling weak or weary and if you make a mistake - to pick you up and dust you off so you can start again. My prayer is that you will sense Jesus' companionship along the way, even me - cheering you on.

The Promised Land for You

There is a Promised Land for each one of us and it isn't *in the far off, by and by* somewhere… The Promised Land is attainable here. It is mentioned a great deal in Scripture both as a physical location and metaphorically, in the sense that the Lord always has something ahead of us that is better - something that He always wants to bring breakthrough for us in (Micah 2:13).[2] Jesus always wants to take us higher. He wants us to breakthrough into our land of promise. You can almost add on to that phrase, "your dreams fulfilled, your desire satisfied, your vision realised" or whatever else it might be. What is for certain, it is [even] better than where you are right now!

But Scripture talks about another land, the 'wilderness land' and the wilderness land is the path you have to travel through to reach your Promised Land. The interesting thing about the landscape as we compare the biblical account of Israel with the destiny God has for each one of us, is that our wilderness experience is actually *in* our Promised Land. So, you can be encouraged that whatever you are going through today, it is part of the promise! "Oh no! what do you mean by that" you may exclaim? It means that there is the potential for everything in our lives, even the struggles and hardships, to be used in order to help us reach our destiny. So the world and all that you might be facing is not something to be resisted or to be considered bad. Whatever it is that this season is bringing up in our lives, it is an opportunity to go to a greater place, a greater glory and play a greater part as we move through. So, no matter what it is, the Lord wants you to press on, rejoicing. Embrace the journey.

Jump In

I recall sitting at the edge of a swimming pool with a friend some years ago. I was desperate to learn how to dive in. I can jump in feet first and I am a fairly confident swimmer. I can also hold on for a good thirty minutes treading water. I know this from school competitions! But to dive in headfirst is another thing altogether. My friend also encouraged me to learn to ski and the same is true. Standing at the top of a mountain ski run if you're not very confident knowing that there's only one way down, is pretty scary. If you just stay there, you become paralysed with fear of taking that first step, whilst at the same time contemplating the fact that sooner or later you are going to have to do it. You may be feeling like that right now about this book you have in your hands! Perhaps you're thinking, "I've committed to doing this, I want to do it and I want it to be successful" - so just jump in! Go all out. Commit to the 35 days and see what the Lord will do.

Declare to yourself: *I am ready to determine my direction because I want to move forward with increased freedom and greater joy. I want to travel with friends taking the same road. I want to determine my direction to lead me to a better place.*

Let's go forward with focus, one step at time - little by little taking the ground. Enjoy the journey!

DAY TWO

Overcoming Obstacles

There are often obstacles that we have to face and deal with in order to achieve or accomplish something new. In moving forward there may be thresholds to cross, barriers to break, limiting beliefs that hold you in place. If you feel any sense of dissatisfaction for where you are right now, then you are ready for your Promised Land. You are a candidate for progress, advancement and breakthrough.

Let's consider some familiar obstacles. In our examination, let's tear down the structure, pick apart the power it exerts and dethrone its authority. By this you win and advance through it, after all, that's what this is all about - moving forward as you *determine your direction*.

> *For though we walk in the flesh, we do not war according to the flesh. For the weapons of our warfare are not carnal but mighty in God for pulling down strongholds, casting down arguments and every high thing that exalts itself against the knowledge of God, bringing every thought into captivity to the obedience of Christ.*
> *(2 Corinthians 10:3-5)*

Fear

Fear will stop us from moving forward, if we allow it. It may be because of past experiences. It could be through someone else projecting their fear upon us. Fear can so paralyse that over time it can feel like there is just no way out or forward. Our enemy, fear, is a robber of destiny, fulfilment and success. God has not designed us to live under its rule.

> *For God has not given us a spirit of fear, but of power and of love and of a sound mind.*
> *(2 Timothy 1:7)*

I know what it is like to be gripped with fear. The night before scheduled school trips, I would hear my mother's prophecies of doom of what could and might happen. She never wanted me to partake on trips and her fears would rob me of any sense of anticipation and adventure I could have experienced, which all the other kids seemed to share. Over time, I realised that it was easier for me to see the negative in the future through a negative lens than all the wonder and possibilities of what could lie ahead.

The Lord always has a plan and it is always good! So why wouldn't his arch enemy try to steal that away? It's time to deal with the fears and anxiety, by being persuaded about the Lord's good plans and by seeing the future for what it really is.

> *For I know the **thoughts**[3] that I think toward you, says the LORD, thoughts of peace and not of evil, to give you a future and a hope. (Jeremiah 29:11)*

> *The thief does not come except to steal, and to kill, and to destroy. I have come that they may have life, and that they may have it more abundantly. I am the good shepherd. The good shepherd gives His life for the sheep.*
> *(John 10:10-11)*

Interestingly we read in the same discourse above, where Jesus is teaching his disciples about the life stealer and the robber of joy, that He intentionally assures us He is the One Who can offer us secure leadership into new, safe, and very good pasture land. This ought to encourage you and me to let go of our fears and launch out into the deep and overcome! Yes, overcome the obstacles!

Indecision

Should I go this way or that way? Ever asked yourself that question? Many people think that life is to be lived on a tight rope, that we must stick with the plan or that idea, with no discussion or room to breathe.

Determine Your Direction

One of the greatest gifts we have is choice and free will. There are lots of decisions presented to us in life, but we can sometimes just get stuck because either we're too scared to be flexible, or we're just too afraid to climb out of our trench.

For some people, it can be indecision that holds them captive, thus hindering forward motion. Similarly, too much analysis and thought processing can be an obstacle. It has been said, "too much analysis leads to paralysis"[4] so if you are constantly trying to work it all out - thinking about the 'what ifs' and 'maybes', STOP!! Breathe and simply choose. If it helps, perhaps write all your options on a piece of paper, close your eyes, shuffle them up and ask Jesus to be in the one you pick! Then run with it and don't look back. Trust Jesus to be in this with you.

Realise that not all questions will be answered for us on this side of eternity. My encouragement to you for now is to overcome your obstacles.

Procrastination

Sometimes procrastination is just plain old laziness - we need to be ruthless and recognise it for what it is! I have tolerated procrastination for too long, allowing it to affect so many areas of my life. How about you? Are you putting off the inevitable, hoping that it will go away, or that another alternative will be offered? The Lord wants you to *seize the day* with Him. Run to the start line. Action that one small task and you're underway. The following Scripture can be applied to this very obstacle:

> *The lazy person claims, "There's a lion on the road! Yes, I'm sure there's a lion out there!" As a door swings back and forth on its hinges, so the lazy person turns over in bed. Lazy people take food in their hand but don't even lift it to their mouth. Lazy people consider themselves smarter than seven wise counselors.*
> *(Proverbs 26:13-16, NLT)*

Laziness should not be part of our life, our thinking or our vocabulary, if we truly want to move forward. It takes effort to move. It takes effort to get started, but once you have begun the journey of determining your direction, there is a momentum that builds. Today might just be the kickstart you need to say, "I'm going to get moving no matter how slow it is, or whatever it looks like." Overcome the obstacles!

Possessed by the Past

We may also be passed possessed instead of forward focused. We can be constantly looking at yesterday and what took place. This can stop us from seeing a future open up ahead. If this resonates with you then today, deal with that regret, that pain, in whatever form it takes. The Holy Spirit knows no bounds in reaching into the past, delivering us from all captivity, as long as we have repented where necessary and released forgiveness into all known situations causing the hurt, pain or loss. To move in the right direction we need to move the opposite way to the wrong one. This is what repentance is. I am sure you have seen the slogan, "don't look back, you're not going that way!"[5]

Take Care with What You Hear

Words are very powerful and can ring in our ears, shape our decisions, and direct our hearts and actions, long after they have been released. Words are sent on a mission - that is why we have to not only be careful what we say, but we have to be careful what we *hear*. Hearing and listening are two different things. I can listen, but not hear. I can know that something has been said, but I can choose to take note or disregard it. I wish someone had helped me to see this years ago.

If there are binding, restrictive, confining and enslaving words that hinder your forward motion, then take action now! Forgive and release whoever spoke them, even if that is yourself. Repent and say sorry to God for agreeing with those words and for allowing them to *determine your direction*. Shake them off, break them off in the name above all names, Jesus Christ, and if necessary, have someone stand with you to pray them off. It then may be necessary to reframe your mindset by speaking out the opposite in declaration (see Romans 12:2).[6] This is so powerful. Speak things over your future that indicates where you want to go, what you want to see, what you can believe for and how your future should shape up. Take a moment to do this now. By doing so, you are already overcoming the obstacles.

Lack of Vision

Vision is a motivator. It can propel us forward and generate energy. When you just can't see a way forward, you can pray for wisdom and revelation. As you take time out to meditate and wait upon the Lord, you can think about where you are heading, what direction is your life pointing toward, and ask yourself what do you really want in the future. Lack of vision can be an obstacle, but it can so easily be overcome. Whatever might be in the way, as a roadblock, the Lord wants you to move forward through it and He offers you everything necessary to do so.

> *If any of you lacks wisdom, let him ask of God, who gives to all liberally and without reproach, and it will be given to him. But let him ask in faith, with no doubting, for he who doubts is like a wave of the sea driven and tossed by the wind.*
> *(James 1:5-6, NKJV)*

Determine Your Direction

(I) do not cease to give thanks for you, making mention of you in my prayers: that the God of our Lord Jesus Christ, the Father of glory, may give to you the spirit of wisdom and revelation in the knowledge of Him, the eyes of your understanding being enlightened; that you may know what is the hope of His calling, what are the riches of the glory of His inheritance in the saints, and what is the exceeding greatness of His power toward us who believe, according to the working of His mighty power.
(Ephesians 1:16-19)

> *"Energy and persistence conquers all things"*
> *Benjamin Franklin*[7]

That is a good quote, however I think to "conquer all things" demands a little more than just energy and persistence, albeit they are certainly a dynamic duo for making things happen. It is my desire to impart some energy and thrust to you as you as you work through this devotional, to help you *determine your direction.*

The key is to think on truth. The words that Jesus said are true. As Christians, He is our leader and He is the one Whom we should be looking to for our direction. Jesus came on a mission with purpose and His life is the inspiration for us all.

*For **this purpose,** the Son of God was manifested, that He might destroy the works of the devil.*
(1 John 3:8)

*For this cause I was born, and for **this cause** I have come into the world, that I should bear witness to the truth. Everyone who is of the truth hears My voice."*
(John 18:38)

We too, can have that same sense of purpose in our lives every single day; the same sense of meaning that helps propel us forward and give us momentum for our future. Why don't you ask the Lord for a renewed vision of your future right now? Write down what you sense Him saying to you.

Perfectionism

The Merriam-Webster Dictionary online defines of *perfectionism* as "a disposition to regard anything short of perfection as unacceptable.[8] This is another obstacle that can hold us up - if we think everything has to be just right before we make a move. I recently heard these liberating words from a friend…***done beats perfect!*** In other words, do your best and in all things look for excellence, but realise that things do not have to be perfect to be good, life-giving, fruitful and successful.

Determine Your Direction

Perfectionism has led to depression, anxiety, eating disorders and other negative behaviours, in many lives. According to the medically accredited online source *VeryWellMind.com*, an obvious and common trait of a person considered to have a 'perfectionist' nature is someone who tends "to spot mistakes and imperfections," with a tendency to be "more judgemental and hard on themselves and on others when 'failure' does occur."[9] Perfection's partnership with pride is evident…yet at the same time, so is its connection with shame and fear. We all make mistakes. No one - other than Jesus, has made it through life without some error! We have all fallen short somewhere along the road. You are not alone.

The key is rising up from any mistake, inaccuracy or failure and taking the yoke of humility to see that you can fail and rise, and fail and rise again. It is OK to fail in the trying! If perfectionism has been driving you - stop! Repent, receive grace and move on:

For the lovers of God may suffer adversity and stumble seven times, but they will continue to rise over and over again. But the unrighteous are brought down by just one calamity and will never be able to rise again.
(Proverbs 24:16 TPT)

For a righteous man may fall seven times and rise again, but the wicked shall fall by calamity.
(Proverbs 24:16 NKJV)

Taking hold of these Scriptures just read, I encourage you to throw off the heavyweights and run free today. To "face off" any obstacles that lie in your path, which are hindering you determining your direction. Throughout this 35-day journey, you are going to be strengthened in lots of areas. You will know joy and freedom as you advance forward.

Stand fast therefore in the liberty by which Christ has made us free, and do not be entangled again with a yoke of bondage (captivity).
(Galatians 5:1)

You Are a Winner

The Lord has not set you up to fail, but to win. What is the meaning of a winner? A winner always contributes to solutions. The loser is always part of the problem. The winner always has a plan, the loser always has an excuse. Don't *make* any excuses today, choose to *move* them right out of the way! Smash the excuses, the procrastination, whatever it might be that is holding you back. Declare yourself to be ***an overcomer*** of every obstacle! Amen!

DAY THREE

Attitude

"I can't change my feelings," is a big lie. You can change your attitude to what is going on in you and around you. From negative to positive and from bad to good! Your attitude goes a long way to *determining your direction* and influencing your *feelings* and *emotions*.

I have always been interested and intrigued by air travel. In fact I did get through the selection process to join the cabin crew of *Monarch Airlines* when their brand new 757 was launched. It was a change of career that I was seeking for all the wrong reasons at that season in my life, needless to say, I didn't actually follow through. However, the dream to fly away and visit places like USA, Australia, Europe ever increased. To date, I've travelled and been in more than twenty-eight different countries and have lost count how many times I've been to the USA. So all those dreams have been fulfilled. Yet air travel still intrigues me. How does all that metal, all those passengers and crew, all their bags and packages, all the drinks and food get off the ground safely? It is all explained by physics: The wing of the aircraft's downward push results in an equal and opposite push back upward, causing lift. The speed, the thrust and the position of the wings of the aircraft all contribute. We don't particularly watch for all these factors, but we trust they all work perfectly because of the laws that are in motion. The aircraft has to be in the right position and balance. For this each aircraft has an *attitude indicator*. The attitude indicator informs the pilot of the aircraft's orientation relative to Earth's horizon, and gives an indication of the smallest orientation change the instant it occurs.

In a similar way, we should live in the right position and balance and interestingly, it is our attitude that displays this.

Our attitude determines our perspectives and responses. As believers in Jesus Christ, Ephesians chapter 2 verse 6 says that we are seated together with Him in heavenly places.[10] Let us take a moment to understand what this is saying… If we take hold of this truth and choose to apply it to ourselves, it means we have access to gain a perspective from a higher position; to see and understand with the very mind of Christ! (See 1 Corinthians 2:16.)

Similarly, to flying an aircraft, our attitude can actually be the vehicle to move us forward and upward, give lift and momentum and propel us to where we want to be.

Aptitude is all to do with competency. How good we are at doing things. Attitude is something that is determined by heart and choice. So if people have the right mindset they can be both motivated and adaptable, which makes them more pliable when it comes to learning new things. Our attitude is under our control. We must take responsibility for the way we choose to think. Our thoughts can actually influence our feelings. So, we can come through any circumstance if we make the choice to gain and maintain the right attitude.

Toll Booth Story

Here is a great story about a guy on a road trip in San Francisco: He came to a toll road where there were seventeen toll booths. As he approached the row of booths, he could see that the toll-collector inside his particular booth was dancing. Intrigued, he asked what he was doing. The man replied, "I'm having a party." Pointing to the other sixteen booths, the driver asked why they were just sitting down in theirs. The man said, "they're not invited to my party." He continued to dance whilst waiting on the driver for his toll money.

After some time he needed to pass that way again and on approaching the toll booths, looked to see if he could find the same collector. Sure enough there he was, standing out amongst the others. The driver exclaimed, "You're the guy I saw dancing the last time I was passing

Determine Your Direction

through and you're still here dancing! Tell me - what do you make of all your colleagues?" "Well," replied the toll-collector, "what do they look like to you? To me, they are vertical coffins and I can prove it." He went on to explain. "At 8:30 every morning, people get in their booth and they die for eight hours. Then at 4:30 in the afternoon, like Lazarus from the dead, they re-emerge and go home for eight hours. Their brain is on hold, dead on the job...going through the motions."

This toll-collector had developed a positive attitude toward his job. He decided he was going to make his job count by the approach that he had. The driver asked one more question to the toll-collector. He queried, "Why do you do what you do?" He replied, "I'm glad you asked that. One day, I'm going to be a dancer." With that, he looked up and pointing to the administration building not far away said, "My bosses are in there and they're paying for my training!"

Do you like that story? I love it! There's sixteen people dying in their job and the seventeenth, in precisely the same situation, figured out a way to live! He was having a party by his approach and attitude!

The story continues... Later on, the driver invited him out for lunch. In the midst of their conversation the man suddenly said, "I don't understand why anybody would think my job is boring. I have a corner office, glass on all sides, I can see the Golden Gate Bridge, San

Attitude

Francisco, the Berkeley Hills. Half of the Western World take their holidays here and I just stroll in every day and practice dancing!"

The author of this story is unknown, but when I stumbled upon it I just had to share it. This man made his mind up to be happy and forward thinking no matter what and we can do the same. So my challenge to you today is no matter what you're facing in your life or how mundane a day looks to you right now, *determine your direction* by having a great attitude.

DAY FOUR

Believe for Breakthrough

What comes to mind when you hear the word **breakthrough?** Breakthrough isn't always a brick wall in front of us that we have to hammer down or take ages to shift. Breakthrough can be in a simple change of mindset, thought pattern, or as straightforward as shifting what you're focusing on. Breakthroughs can come in so many different ways, but you have to believe *beyond* what you can see. This is the definition of 'living by faith'. We believe for breakthrough by creating a different time frame in our thinking. Let me explain what I mean. Just last evening we had an amazing worship gathering in church. We began to sing spontaneously and prophetically. In the midst of the worship we declared over and over again the phrase from the Lord's prayer, "Hallowed be Your Name."

After singing this for a while, we moved onto the next line, "Your Kingdom come on earth as it is in heaven." Our repetitive declaration created an atmosphere of faith that lifted us to the place where we could receive an 'Heaven to Earth' perspective. That is, looking at Earth from God's viewpoint. When we think about determining our direction obviously we're looking at where we want to get to… We are thinking about what lies ahead of us. So as we consider being "seated with Christ" and being empowered to see what He sees (see *Day 3*), it really can be as simple as turning our heads *from-here-to-there* in the natural. Translate this action into the spiritual and our vision becomes a *from-Heaven-to-Earth* perspective. Applying this mindset with faith by believing and declaring the Word of God, we can activate our future now and pull it into our present.

Several years ago, shortly after being married, myself and husband Steve were living in a small village. It was here - in the small - that I cultivated big dreams and received great vision for my future. There were things that I wanted to achieve, to see and do. There were dreams that seemed impossible and out of reach in that season of my life. In my day-dreaming, I can remember sitting at home and thinking about where I would like to be in five years time. Have you ever done that? Before you know it, your thoughts have gone far beyond where you are in the moment. As I day-dreamed, suddenly a thought captivated me, *… If I were there [in my future] now, accomplishing and achieving all those things that I can see in my spirit, then why am I sitting here dressed like this?*

Without hesitation I went to my wardrobe and changed the clothes I was wearing. Now it wasn't as if I had a model wardrobe to choose from, it was a simple act (in faith) of what I could believe for and what I could believe to be doing. I just changed one thing that I could, in response to the change in my thinking.

Time moved on, I forgot all about the incident. We relocated and in the course of time, we joined an international ministry where opportunities to minister opened up for us. Some years in, I suddenly had a memory recall back to the moment when I was dreaming of my future, where I changed my outfit to fit my vision. I promptly realised I was actually standing in that very place where I dreamt of being, all those years previously!

My encouragement to you today is to think about where you would like to be in your life in the next year, in the next two years, the next five years and the next ten years, and begin to put yourself into that narrative. Dare to dream with Jesus and begin write your story.

Our thoughts take us somewhere and one thought can be the catalyst to your breakthrough. Every problem you have will be answered either in the future, or now. Every problem that you face has a solution and it is going to be solved either in the future, or in the present. This is a secret few discover, to live not from the past, nor from the present, but live *from* the future. This isn't wishing-your-life-away thinking, neither is it "pie in the sky when we die."[11] This is understanding that we are living in time and space where we can actually taste the powers of the age to come in the very place that we are today.

The secret is to live *not from the problem*. You can choose to live - not from your present crisis, rather from a vision of its future victory. This is the word for you today: Live not from your present obstacle, but from your future breakthrough!!

If you feel like you are in a war zone, the battle you are facing is already won by Christ in your future. So don't live from the battle, live from your future victory.

When you are asking for something in prayer, give thanks - even before seeing the breakthrough. This is faith and Hebrews chapter 11 tells us that faith pleases God - God is able! Seat yourself with Jesus and live from heavens perspective, from the kingdom yet to come, from the life yet to be, even from the you that you are yet to become! Believe for breakthrough by learning the secret of living from the future, in your present.

DAY FIVE

Choose Your Company

'Life-joints' are those precious relationships that make the journey bearable, worthwhile and fulfilling! We are made to relate. How are you investing in others, receiving from others and sharing the burdens of others? People come and go, some stay forever. Think about who is part of your journey at this season of your life.

Choosing the company we travel with is important. Not just associations with individuals whom we brush up against once in a while, but the people that really matter, who become precious to us. We don't get to choose every relationship that lands in our path, for instance, the family that we are born into. You could be an only child with few family relationships, or part of a large family with many siblings and with an extended family. We don't get to choose the associates and colleagues we work alongside, unless of course you're the boss! However, there are many relationships where we *can* choose who to bring up close and into our personal space, or to keep on the fringe and just say "hi" and "bye" to now and again - that is also fine. Relations of all these kinds are important. Every relationship matters.

Determine Your Direction

We can place relationships into three general categories:

1. Those who relate to us because they need what we carry: These are people who need *who* you are. They need the special gifts and gift-mix that is uniquely you. Some people come into our lives because they need us to make an investment into them. It gives me great joy when I see someone I have encouraged take a new step, or reach a goal, or a person I have coached being emboldened to do something for the first time. I *like* to encourage people on their journey and I *want* to invest my life into them.

2. There are peer relationships, which are equal - where we can give and receive from each other. We need these 'life-joints' relationships to help us determine our direction.

3. Further to these, there are those we look to for our forward and upward momentum. Those who spur us on, supplying us with energy, drive and inspiration. They instill hope and vision. We need those relationships that we can look to for coaching or mentoring. They are walking a path beyond ours and holding their hand out, inviting us to walk with them.

Who we are associated with, or aligned to, really does make a difference in determining our direction.

Choose Your Company

"Who you are running with, is where you are running to."
(Author unknown)

Think about those people in your life that are going somewhere and who have their eye on a goal, a vision, a prize. A person you know who has direction and discipline. Choose to get alongside them, shoulder to shoulder and remember - a good relationship meets both ways. You can also be one that brings others on, too. Be a giver first and you will find others giving themselves into your life.

John Maxwell, the amazing seasoned life coach, said that when you encounter those difficult people in your life - the ones who always seem to rub you up the wrong way - what you need to do is, instead of rejecting them, put an imaginary number "10" on their forehead as you greet them. Think of this person as ten-out-of-ten. Learn to value everyone. Look and see the treasure, even in the difficult and seemingly unmanageable relationships.

Now if you really want to take it a step further and see how important they are, you can take the advice of Bishop Bill Hamon from Christian International, Florida. He says for every person that causes a disagreeable reaction within us, we should send a note of thanks or a gift of appreciation, thanking them for the deeper work of grace that they have initiated in our heart and life! Consider for a moment how that person working on your nerves like sandpaper, is the one sent by the Lord to produce more love, grace and patience, providing the catalyst for you to actually move forward! Even if you have some relationships that are hard work, see the value in them. If you respond rightly, you will be benefited by them.

Life is all about relationships and the company that we keep. In relationships, we give and we receive. We serve and we love. You are growing by your giving, you are learning by your loving, you are sowing by your serving. It is written by God in His laws of nature that you cannot sow without reaping. So finally you are rising…as you receive.

Evaluate the relationships that you have in your life. Without rejecting anyone, just consider who you are giving in to, who you are receiving from each one and how you can add more value to the lives of others. Be a giver, not a taker. Be a lover of people and be a server. Be a sower into the lives around you. The outcome will be the rebounding of more love, joy, peace, patience, kindness, goodness, faithfulness and gentleness in your life (Galatians 5:22-23). You will find yourself heading in the right direction, as you benefit and bless others.

DAY SIX

What Delights You?

I do so enjoy travel! Whether long distance to warmer climates or nearby for a good outdoor hike. Sometimes on these jaunts we have to consult the trusty old compass to point us in the right direction.

Are you aware that there is an inward compass that you can consult when you are trying to navigate your way forward through life's seasons? A great question to ask yourself when seeking your next step is, "what *delights* you?"

The compass of our heart is set by what we take delight in. Mike Bickle from IHOP-KC has written a book called *The Seven Longings of The Human Heart*.[12] He outlines how each one of us is made for greatness and for beauty. He explains how there are deep longings within every individual to be wholehearted and to make a deep and lasting impact in life. I encourage you to lean in to these divinely placed longings inside your heart, as you *determine your direction*.

What are those dreams and aspirations that make you want to get out of bed in the morning? What makes your heart glad? You might want to think about this for a moment and note down what gives you the greatest sense of fulfilment and joy in your life right now.

~ Selah ~

You are already designed and pre-wired with longings, which should point your heart towards seeking God. They are intricately woven into the fabric of your being so that you will search for Him and upon finding Him, be fully satisfied in Him. Furthermore, the outworking of these longings will establish your path, your career, your hobbies and interests. If Jesus is in the centre of your longings, they will lead to fulfilment and contentment.

As surely as Genesis 1:27 says that we are made in the image of our Creator, so we are all made with the longing to be enjoyed by Him. Why? Because we are made by a wonderful God who is a Father to us, who loves us, and wants relationship with us. If we are having a low-esteem day, it can be hard to admit to ourselves that we do really want to be connected to and enjoyed by Him. The truth is, every ***"ah ah"*** epiphany that elicits wonder and joy in us…the powerful moments that take our breath away, that fascinate us, surprise us… All are gifts from our kind heavenly Father in order for us to realise we are enjoyed by Him.

What Delights You

Many of us find that there are things we do in life because we have to do them, rather than our heart being in it. Steve and I were talking about this with friends around the meal table. The discussion turned to cooking, not my greatest strength! My friend was suggesting that the difference between a good meal and a really exceptional meal is the care that you take over preparing and cooking it. I thought that was great advice, because when you care about what you are doing you put your whole heart into it. You can literally taste the love! Being wholehearted is a key when you are looking to *determine your direction*.

One of the most impacting life stories to me, is that of Eric Henry Liddell. The account of his life is told through the 1981 Oscar winning movie, ***Chariots of Fire.***[13]

Eric was a Scottish sprinter, rugby player, and Christian missionary. To quote from Wikipedia, "born in Qing, China to Scottish missionary parents, he attended boarding school near London. He spent time, when possible, with his family in Edinburgh, and afterwards attended the University of Edinburgh… At the 1924 Summer Olympics in Paris, Liddell refused to run in the heats for his favoured 100 metres because they were held on a Sunday. Instead, he competed in the 400 metres held on a weekday, a race that he won. He returned to China in 1925 to serve as a missionary teacher. Aside from two furloughs in Scotland, he remained in China until his death in a Japanese civilian internment camp in 1945."[14]

Champion runner Eric was a believer. He loved God. In the film's dialogue at one point he was being reprimanded by his sister for neglecting his responsibilities before God as he devoted his focus toward competitive running. His response was" I believe that God made me for a purpose. But He also made me fast, and **when I run, I feel His pleasure**."

Think about the longings of your heart that can help you move forward. You have a good, good Father who wants you to reach your destiny. He wants you to partner with Him to *determine your direction* in life, so that you can arrive at your destination.

DAY SEVEN

Selah Reflection:

Understanding Shabbat Rest

Shabbat is the Jewish and Biblical rest. Some denominations teach that in Jesus, we have already entered into God's rest and, therefore, no longer need to observe Shabbat. Of course, resting in Jesus' finished work is of vital importance. One of the paramount blessings is to discover that Jesus has truly won the victory and we need only to trust in Him. Every believer needs to enter that type of 'rest' in Him. Nevertheless, even if we understand all that Jesus did for us and experience His 'rest' spiritually, we can still can become physically and emotionally exhausted.

God wants to bless us in every area of life and is not just concerned with us spiritually. He wants us to enter His rest not just in a *theological* sense, but in a way that we can physically experience His presence and joy at least one day of every week. Therefore, God has designated times for you and your family to rest and be restored. These are times set aside for you to appreciate fully and relish His goodness. These are times to regain strength, to be refreshed and restored. He wants us to take time to stop and remember that He is good.

To rest is God's will for us. He designed our bodies to shut down and sleep for several hours a day. Times of daily rest recharge our bodies in order to maintain the stamina we need to fulfil His purposes. This concept of rest is so important to God that The Lord included the weekly Sabbath in the ten commandments.[15]

To break from the pattern and to introduce this concept, I am inviting you to use the following questions to reflect, meditate, evaluate and review the last six days, rather than absorb and concentrate on just taking-in more information.

1. Can you identify your Promised Land? Is there something or somewhere on your horizon that is just out of reach today? Take a few moments to consider what you would change right now, if it were possible to do so.

2. Take time to focus on the six chapters you have just read. Let your heart and spirit soar in worship. From that perspective begin to see and believe again that with God all things are possible.

Selah Reflection: Understanding Shabbat Rest

3. Identify any obstacles that hinder you from moving forward and make a commitment to deal with them. Ask the Lord to show you how and if necessary, reach out and ask someone for help and prayer.

4. Use this time to give thanks for all the relationships and friends that have contributed to your life and that currently bring joy, security, affirmation and peace to you.

DAY EIGHT

Encounters

First encounters and first impressions! How easy is it for you to be the first to introduce yourself? Do you wait to be approached, or are you the one to make the initial move?

We are changed by each and every encounter we have. There is a potential friendship in every new handshake! I am always expectant and hopeful to make friends with someone new - how about you?

We have thought about the company that we choose and the relationships that become precious to us over time. Often, such friendships stay alongside us through life, sharing in our joys and sorrows. However, before we can get to that place of deep friendship that endures, we have to *first encounter them.*

For someone to really make a difference in our life, we have to be up close and personal. However, we can scarcely tell by the first meeting whether or not that person will be part of the journey long term, or whether they will make any kind of impact on our lives at all.

To 'encounter' means *to meet, to stumble upon and to experience*. I am referring in this section to **unexpected first impressions**. Someone, or something, that potentially could have a life changing impact in our lives.

Just one touch can change everything

There is a phrase used in forensic investigations, "every touch leaves a trace."[16] Wow! If we could re-think our casual 'meet and greets' and see them as potential connections for purpose, we may approach people very differently.

It is always exciting to me to meet new people. I have the privilege of experiencing this all the time in the ministry field that I am in. There really are so many opportunities for each one of us to mingle. You may feel you need to brush up on greeting skills, role-play introductory conversations, making eye contact, or simply smiling and saying "Hello, it's nice to meet you!"

As believers, we can think about the encounters that we have with the Lord. Remember that first encounter that changed you forever? How Jesus graciously made Himself known to you… How He melted your heart and baptised you with His love and fiery passion… No doubt He has continued to draw you again and again calling deep to deep, releasing over you rivers of revelation as He shares His heart. Truly this is His desire. Even in the wilderness seasons and dry places of your life, in His love, Jesus finds a way to chase you down and vanquish your heart. He is the one Who will direct your compass eternally and set the course for your eternal destination.

But what about on a daily basis? In the here and now? Sometime ago during a season of transition in our lives, we joined a certain ministry organisation. I remember the leader taking us under her wing and saying some very profound things to us, as we embarked on this unchartered new venture with her. This is one of the impactful things she said, "I'm going to coach you, not counsel you, and I'm going to direct you not disciple you, because I am not your pastor - I am your mentor."

In those four years season of receiving mentoring and coaching, I learned such a lot of things. During [our] time there, I never felt constrained or manipulated. Whenever we had discussions regarding life choices, she always presented me with options and although the most beneficial path was abundantly clear, so was my choice to whether I would take it or not. A good mentor, like the one I had, always gives you options and gives you the freedom to choose.

Remember, every chance meeting and each new friend has the potential

Determine Your Direction

to become one of the company you run with. I would like to put it this way… There are no chance meetings if God is directing your life! There are only God 'appointments', God 'coincidences' and divine connections. This is what you are looking for on your journey. As you *determine your direction*, watch out for those *divine connections*.

Moses was ***changed*** as He encountered God's Presence. So much so that His skin actually shone (Exodus 34:30). King David was healed as he beheld the Lord:

> *One thing I have desired of the LORD, that will I seek: that I may dwell in the house of the LORD all the days of my life, to behold the beauty of the LORD, and to inquire in His temple.*
> *(Psalm 27:4)*

Expect life to flow into you as you get into God's presence and *behold the Lord*. Reach out to greet new people today.

Determine Your Direction

DAY NINE

Forgiveness

Foundations are the starting position of any building work. They are very important and the depth of the foundations determine the height and size of the structure being erected. One very important foundation that we need to lay in our lives, which gives us momentum throughout and enables us to "finish" our race well, is forgiveness.

When children are growing up and learning to live at peace with their friends, they are often taught to apologise, to say "sorry" when they have wronged someone. A playground spat or a jealous outburst is all part of growing up, but do we really teach the fundamentals of forgiveness?

Forgiveness originates in God's heart. It is something He initiated and demonstrated by sending His Son to die in our place. There was an offence, there was a payment, there was restitution. It includes repentance, in order for true reconciliation to take place.

Forgiveness is a flow that we can live in. A flow that we can move in all the time. It is a gift from God. I am sure you can recall being hurt, offended, or violated. We all have to learn to forgive. It isn't a natural response. It is a supernatural response. Sometimes it is really difficult. It may take some time to reach the place of true surrender in order to truly forgive someone. The good news is that it is possible! If we don't live in the flow of forgiveness, we can get clogged up. We develop an issue if we are unable to forgive. Unforgiveness towards others actually ends up damaging us more.

It is a great foundation, because it keeps us in the flow of moving forward. If you want to determine a good way ahead then make sure you are in the flow. Take time to let the Lord heal any hurts or pain - giving it all to Him. Forgive and release any and all who have wronged you.

As I was preparing and asking the Lord Jesus to give me a fresh word for this day, He said to me, "Breathe and relax…" So I did. I paused and just waited, until He spoke again. He said, "Let Me take the strain. However, the only way to do that, is to let Me take the reins."

Now I'm not a horse owner, rider or lover, but I am a horse respecter. I do respect this wonderful breed of animal, and I love to observe from a distance. I did try horse riding once and soon realised it wasn't for me. However, I learnt just how important the bridle and the reins attached

Forgiveness

to the head and the neck of the horse are. It only takes a very slight movement of the hand of the rider to actually guide that horse. It knows whether to stop, to start, to go right or to go left, because it has learned the reins of the master.

We have to allow ourselves to be in a place where we can let the Lord of our lives "take the strain" of our lives, by giving him the reins. Think about what the word *strain* implies for a moment. When we strain a muscle through over-exertion, it is very painful. Putting strain into the context of emotional, spiritual or mental stress can become a serious hinderance to our forward movement. Let the Lord take the reins today! Become quick to release forgiveness and grace to others.

So let the foundation of forgiveness be laid today. It might feel like a fight within you. Maybe you are in that moment of struggle to forgive and release someone, or you may even need to forgive yourself. Take encouragement from the Apostle Paul:

> *I have fought the good fight, I have finished the race, I have kept the faith. Finally, there is laid up for me the crown of righteousness, which the Lord, the righteous Judge, will give to me on that Day, and not to me only but also to all who have loved His appearing. (2 Timothy 4:7-8)*

Determine Your Direction

You can lay this good foundation and live in the joy of it. You can experience it propelling you forward as you *determine your direction* and you can be assured that it will enable you to finish your race well.

> *For I know the thoughts that I think toward you, says the LORD, thoughts of peace and not of evil, to give you a future and a hope. (Jeremiah 29:11)*

God has good plans for you and an adventure.

DAY TEN

Grow Up and You Will Go Up

Surely, we all want to grow?

Anything with life in it grows and develops. When God created the trees, plants and vegetation, He spoke to the earth. When He created the birds and flying creatures and insects, He spoke to the heavens. But when God created mankind, He sculpted from the dust of the ground and spoke to Himself saying, "Let Us make man in Our image." Kneeling, He *breathed* His breath of life into the first man… Adam.

Just as all other *living* things need their original environment to continue growing in, so we too, need to be rightly connected to our original source in order to flourish. Cut a flower from its root and eventually it dies. Take a fish out of its natural habitat and it eventually dies. Do you get the picture? Stay connected and close to your source and the obvious result will be life and growth. The question we need to ask ourselves is, *are we growing*? The baby stage is cute and exciting as new discoveries are made and stages of growth are accomplished, but no one wants to stay at the baby stage all through their life.

Determine Your Direction

The process of growth is dependent on various conditions. For instance, the ageing process is dependent on time. We grow intellectually based on our education. The process of spiritual maturity, becoming more and more like the Lord, has everything to do with obedience! Ouch! Jesus learned obedience by the things he suffered.

> *Though He was a Son, yet He learned obedience by the things which He suffered. And having been perfected, He became the author of eternal salvation to all who obey Him,*
> *(Hebrews 5:8-9)*

Jesus used the "Parable of the Sower"[17] to warn that immaturity would result from seeking pleasures of the world, rather than seeking the Kingdom of God:

> *Now the ones that fell among thorns are those who, when they have heard, go out and are choked with cares, riches, and pleasures of life, and bring no fruit to maturity.*
> *(Luke 8:14)*

> *However, we speak wisdom among those who are mature, yet not the wisdom of this age, nor of the rulers of this age, who are coming to nothing. But we speak the wisdom of God in a mystery, the hidden wisdom which God ordained before the ages for our*

glory.
(1 Corinthians 2:6-7)

My little children, for whom I labor in birth again until Christ is formed in you...
(Galatians 4:19)

No one likes the look, or stench, of a stagnant pool, where the water does not flow freely. Stay fresh, stay updated and stay flourishing in your pursuit to *determine your direction.*

In order for us to *go up*, we have to *grow up* and so think today about what you are feeding into your life to aid your development. Think about what is healthy, what is fresh and new. You may wish to consider the books you read, or the programmes you watch. Are they helping you grow intellectually? Etcetera.

"Not all readers are leaders, but all leaders are readers"
Harry S. Truman[18]

Give thought today about the people you spend time with and the things you are engaging in. Consider how they help you grow and mature, or not.

DAY ELEVEN

Hurry

Hurry can be a monster - it can steal, kill and destroy our peace, precious relationships and much more if left unrestrained. Enjoy the moments in the day to "stop and smell the roses," as the well-known idiom asserts, and be at peace!

I expect at some point you have heard these words, perhaps even said them to yourself, "hurry up," or "hurry up, get on with it!" (Whatever "it" might be…)

Hurry is one of those things in our life that we have to watch. It can be quite destructive if we're not careful. Hurry stirs up an impatient spirit, which often tends to lead to a manifestation of frustration. If not nipped in the bud early enough, it can end in a display of anger.

At the end of the day, *Hurry is not our friend*. Apart from causing stress on a mind and body level, it can lead to the breakdown of relationships. I have seen impatience lead to anger, where equipment and objects have been thrown and destroyed. Hurry and impatience are not desirable attributes we should entertain.

Take a moment before moving on to think about how much 'hurry' impacts and impinges on your life. Jot down in your journal any thoughts, along with any necessary changes you could make.

~ *Selah* ~

John Mark Comer's book "The Ruthless Elimination of Hurry" (2019), reveals that to get off life's treadmill and actually live at the pace that we are designed to live, you have to be ruthless with *Hurry*.[19] *Ruthless* means to show no mercy. I encourage you to become relentless in gaining mastery in this area. It will be worth it.

My prayer is that the moments of reflection within this devotional are helping you to pause, relax and breathe that little more deeply.

Are you familiar with the movie, *Employee of the Month (2006)?* It is based on the large hypermarkets like *Costco*. Although a comedy, it demonstrates perfectly the pace at which we are all expected to operate at, according to the 'World's' standard. The employee has to frantically scan as many products through the checkout line as possible within a given time, in order to win the accolade. It is both funny and tense at the same time. Yet in the midst of the hurried, frenetic activity, more than just mistakes are made misdemeanours are covered up and the outcome of events wind-up the opposite to what is hoped for. The main moral of the story is… *slow down*.

Time is a precious commodity that we have been given. So as we walk each step along the way, let's look for the good in every moment, forsaking the bad, appreciating the things that are so easily overlooked in the busyness of life.

DAY TWELVE

Instruction

We are all a work in progress - under construction -you might say, but are we prepared and ready to really receive instruction?

> *My son, hear the instruction of your father, and do not forsake the law of your mother.*
> *(Proverbs 1:8)*

> *He also taught me, and said to me: "Let your heart retain my words; keep my commands, and live. Get wisdom! Get understanding! Do not forget, nor turn away from the words of my mouth. Do not forsake her, and she will preserve you; love her, and she will keep you. Wisdom is the principal thing; therefore get wisdom. And in all your getting, get understanding. Exalt her, and she will promote you; she will bring you honour, when you embrace her. She will place on your head an ornament of grace; a crown of glory she will deliver to you."*
> *(Proverbs 4:4-9)*

Determine Your Direction

The excellence of *wisdom* is demonstrated in Proverbs chapter 8. It would be a good exercise to read that now. Wisdom calls out…she has a voice, if we will stop to listen.

There is wisdom, revelation and instruction available for you today. Where do we receive instruction from? Within your answer may be parents, family, friends, education, employers, colleagues, books, movies - anything really that we focus on, listen to and watch. But for wise instruction, we should be thankful. If you consider yourself to have had a good upbringing, if you were given a good education, then you have been blessed to receive wise instruction. You have been provided with good teachers and trainers. The same goes for stepping in to a career. For the first couple of years of my banking profession, I was able to go to college and take other courses to further my knowledge and understanding in subject matters I was more interested in. I am extremely grateful I was able to do so.

We can gain wisdom as we learn from the opportunities and lessons that life affords us and as we ask Jesus to teach us. His Spirit is the greatest Counsellor, Teacher and Revelator we will ever come across. However in order to hear and receive His download, we need to yield to Him by giving time to seek Him, surrendering our heart's will.

The greatest instruction manual we have access to, above all others, is

Instruction

of course the infallible written Word of God, which is unchanging and alive! Wherever you are in life's journey, the Bible Scriptures are applicable and relevant. Many people have testified to the fact that upon simply reading portions of the Scriptures, they have met with, or had a revelation of The Lord Jesus Himself, causing a complete transformation within their thinking, heart and life as a result.

If you are just exploring, or starting out on your relationship with the Lord, I strongly encourage you pick up a Bible and begin reading one of the gospel narratives (the 'books' in the New Testament called Matthew, Mark, Luke and John). These accounts document the life of Jesus. They contain His teaching and instruction for all people - everywhere. Two other books located in the Old Testament that are particularly good for imparting daily instructions are the Psalms and Proverbs. There are thirty-one chapters in the book of Proverbs and it is a good policy to read one chapter a day during a calendar month. The more you meditate on the truths contained, the deeper the impartation - and permeation - of the Word within. The book of Proverbs is an instruction manual in itself and a pattern for living. Proverbs contains amazing instruction, much common sense, loads of encouragement and also that necessary challenge to help us adjust.

Let's pause for a moment before moving on, to consider these questions:

Determine Your Direction

- Where are you getting your instruction from?
- Are you being trained and equipped?
- Are you allowing your direction to be governed by whatever randomly happens?
- Are you making determined strides forward to reach your goals?

There is no better place to put your feet…no steadier place than in the instruction of the Word of The Lord. If you have been on the journey a while, consider whether it is time to refresh your reading program.

Ask the Lord where you should start to meditate for this week, or for this month, and take a fresh approach to His Word every day. Maybe the idea of including a chapter of Proverbs each day could be one… Learn to wait for Him to speak, instruct, challenge and encourage you. I believe there is a fresh impartation for you today. The Spirit of Jesus is ready to refresh and revive His Word to you right now!

Psalm 119 is the longest chapter in the Bible. At 176 verses long, it is written as an 'alphabet-acrostic poem' that is broken into twenty-two stanzas, with each stanza representing one of the twenty-two letters contained in the Hebrew alphabet. It is all about the Word, the instruction, the laws, the ordinances, the statutes and the counsel of God. The mandate of Psalm 119 is to remind us of how God's Way is perfect and how our path becomes secure and perfected, as we choose to walk in His ways.

Your word is very pure; therefore Your servant loves it.
(Psalm 119:140)

Psalm 19:7-11 says this of God's ordinances:

The law of the LORD is perfect, converting the soul; the testimony of the LORD is sure, making wise the simple; the statutes of the LORD are right, rejoicing the heart; the commandment of the LORD is pure, enlightening the eyes; the fear of the LORD is clean, enduring forever; the judgments of the LORD are true and righteous altogether. More to be desired are they than gold, yea, than much fine gold; sweeter also than honey and the honeycomb. Moreover by them Your servant is warned, and in keeping them there is great reward.

Here are a small handful of other Scriptures that Psalm 119:140 above alludes to:

For I proclaim the name of the LORD: Ascribe greatness to our God. He is the Rock, His work is perfect; for all His ways are justice, a God of truth and without injustice; righteous and upright

is He.
(Deuteronomy 32:3-4)

As for God, His way is perfect; the word of the LORD is proven; He is a shield to all who trust in Him.
(Psalm 18:30; 2 Samuel 22:31)

It is God who arms me with strength, and makes my way perfect. He makes my feet like the feet of deer, and sets me on my high places.
(Psalm 18:32-33; 2 Samuel 22:33)[20]

But the path of the just is like the shining sun, that shines ever brighter unto the perfect day.
(Proverbs 4:18)

As you *determine your direction* with the instruction manual of the Scriptures, you will increase in light and in radiance and brightness; you will be able to hear clearly instructions from heaven and know your next step. So *instruction* is the key word for today. Let your heart be instructed and may your spirit be teachable.

DAY THIRTEEN

Joy

Hello WINNER! I can greet you at the beginning of a new day like this, because that is what you are. In fact, you are more than that:

> *Who is he who condemns? It is Christ who died, and furthermore is also risen, who is even at the right hand of God, who also makes intercession for us.* **Who shall separate us from the love of Christ?** *Shall tribulation, or distress, or persecution, or famine, or nakedness, or peril, or sword? As it is written: "For Your sake we are killed all day long; we are accounted as sheep for the slaughter." Yet in all these things* **we are more than conquerors** *through Him who loved us. For I am persuaded that neither death nor life, nor angels nor principalities nor powers, nor things present nor things to come, nor height nor depth, nor any other created thing, shall be able to separate us from the love of God which is in Christ Jesus our Lord.*
> (Romans 8:34-39)

You are made to scale the mountains and overcome the obstacles. You

Determine Your Direction

can jump for joy over the walls of opposition. We all face trials and difficulties, but we can leap forward over them all. Jump into the adventure this day as you *determine your direction!*

> *With your help I can advance against a troop; with my God I can scale a wall.*
> *(2 Samuel 22:30, NIV)*

How is it possible to have the strength and power to overcome? It is through joy. Do we fully appreciate what the Lord has done for each one of us? Once we begin to embrace it, joy floods us. That one ingredient is key to breakthrough and victory. What do the walls represent? Anything that is a challenge or limitation to us. The mountain that seems to be unsurmountable.

By exercising joy in the Lord, we can be assured of triumph!

> *…The joy of the LORD is your strength.*
> *(Nehemiah 8:10, ESV)*

James, the writer of the so-named book in the New Testament, encouraged the believers in this way:

> *Dear brothers and sisters, when troubles of any kind come your*

way, consider it an opportunity for great joy. For you know that when your faith is tested, your endurance has a chance to grow. So let it grow, for when your endurance is fully developed, you will be perfect and complete, needing nothing.
(James 1:2-4, NLT)

We are not promised exclusion from the trials, we are provided with a supernatural solution to take us through, over, around and forward. Jump for joy in the trials and in the obstacles, because you are a winner!

There are many accounts in Scripture where we see the pattern of James 1 outworked. One I'd like to draw from is a period in Israel's history, when the Jews returned from captive Babylon back to their native land.[21] The man in charge of the rebuilding was Zerubbabel, the then governor of Judea. The prophet to Israel at that time was Zechariah. He said this,

So he answered and said to me: "This is the word of the LORD to Zerubbabel: 'Not by might nor by power, but by My Spirit,' says the LORD of hosts. 'Who are you, O great mountain? Before Zerubbabel you shall become a plain! And he shall bring forth the capstone with shouts of "Grace, grace to it!"'" Moreover the word of the LORD came to me, saying: "The hands of Zerubbabel have laid the foundation of this temple; his hands shall also finish it.

> *Then you will know that the LORD of hosts has sent Me to you. For who has despised the day of small things?"*
> *(Zechariah 4:6-10, NKJV)*

What I find particularly interesting in this Scripture is that the mountain is made of stone, but so is the "capstone". The very thing that overcomes the mountain is actually made of the same substance.

As I ponder on this, I believe the Lord is saying that He is going to cause you to be able to overcome the obstacles in your life, by using the very things you consider weaknesses. He will use every obstacle to bring fulfilment to the purposes He has planned, every time. Every crisis, every adversity, every setback, every sorrow will be turned around to bring breakthrough, blessing and triumph.

> *And we know that all things work together for good to those who love God, to those who are the called according to His purpose.*
> *(Romans 8:28)*

Consider the exhilaration of athletic high jumpers as they run with all their might, make one terrific leap with a pole and accomplish a great height! Whatever the obstacle is in front of you today, you can jump for joy remembering that the joy of the Lord is yours to overcome every single circumstance.

Joy

Declare today: *I am determined in this one thing - I am a winner. Whatever comes my way I am going to jump for joy. The devil will not steal my joy because in Jesus Christ, I am a winner!*

DAY FOURTEEN

Selah Reflection: Understanding Shabbat Rest

Rest is a blessing of God.

> *It is vain for you to rise up early, to take rest late, to eat the bread of [anxious] toil - for he gives [blessings] to his beloved in sleep.* (Psalm 127:2, AMPC)

This does not mean you should never get up early or that you must never stay up late. At times this is very necessary. However, the verse does suggest that if you constantly push yourself beyond God's boundaries for your life, you will miss a blessing.

Rest is designed to bless us in many ways, such as physical healing, restoration, mental peace and creativity, as well as emotional rehabilitation.

Determine Your Direction

1. **We all need a strategy for growth.** How are you developing? Think about what input you are receiving… Is it adequate? Should you enrol on a course to equip you, so that you may advance?

2. **Take time to worship the Lord today and ask Him to instruct you.** As you worship Him for His goodness, His righteousness and all He has done for you, meditate on words such as: commandments, statutes, laws, teachings, ordinances, vows, precepts, sayings, testimonies, judgements, asking the Lord for fresh revelation to be imparted to you.

3. **Find ways today to spread joy.** No limits! Let me know how you are inspired and led at jen@bestlifeever.co.uk.

DAY FIFTEEN

Contagious Kindness

Kindness is contagious and is very good for you. It promotes health and well-being, and reduces stress and depression. You can show kindness in lots of ways… D*etermine your direction* today by walking in kindness.

> *But the fruit of the Spirit is love, joy, peace, longsuffering,* **kindness**, *goodness, faithfulness, gentleness, self-control. Against such there is no law.*
> *(Galatians 5:22-23)*

You may have heard the phrase [to do] "random acts of kindness" in which someone spontaneously, even intentionally, steps out to show generosity in a surprising and unexpected way. There are so many benefits to be had if you can engender kindness in your life. The first step to experiencing these benefits is to be grateful towards those who show *you* kindness. In turn, as you reach out in the same way, it causes others to want to do the same. Kindness really is CONTAGIOUS!

Determine Your Direction

I have lots of friends in my life who are kind and generous towards me and I endeavour to release kindness back into their lives. So, step two, as just mentioned, is to release kindness to those you know. Step three, is to look for ways to show compassion that is demonstrating concern for the suffering or misfortunes of others. Some have, where possible, stepped in to pay someone's bill at the supermarket. Of course, that is wonderful but might prove costly. There are many, many ways that cost little or nothing at all to demonstrate kindness and care. For example, you may be able to help in a practical way with a project needing extra hands-on deck, or it might be coming alongside someone to offer support when they need you. You might want to get creative and reach out to new contacts with a 'surprise care package', a simple text greeting or pass on a motivational message. Just reaching out to let someone know you are thinking about them is very powerful.

Smiling is really, really good for you and for those around you. How do you put a smile on somebody else's face? By smiling at them. Try it! You could also attempt making eye contact with someone you don't know and see what reaction you initiate - who knows, they could become your next best friend!!

Complimenting others, sincerely of course, is a great way to spread kindness. It is always good to tell someone they are looking well and to celebrate them. Tell someone you appreciate them today. Say thank you and bless them. As you release the blessing, it will boomerang back. You will end up the recipient of kindness. There is a biblical rule which governs this behaviour, it is referred to as *the law of reciprocity.* We find it in Luke's gospel, chapter 6 verse 38, "Give, and it will be given to you - a good measure, pressed down, shaken together, overflowing, will be given into your lap. For whatever measure you measure out will be measured back to you." (TLV) Whatever you do for or to others, you will find returning to you.

> *See that none of you repays another with evil for evil, but always aim to show kindness and seek to do good to one another and to everybody.*
> *(1 Thessalonians 5:15, AMPC)*

Studies have shown that kindness increases energy levels, which in turn can increase our lifespan. When we are kind to people, it releases the feel-good chemicals and hormones called serotonin and oxytocin. These God-given endocrines are known for decreasing pain, stress, depression and blood pressure.

Showing kindness causes us to think beyond ourselves, giving us the opportunity to be outward focused rather than being self-absorbed. Kindness is an act of giving and is a wonderful gift at our disposal. How will you spend yours today? What random acts of kindness could you do for others to spread joy and happiness? Remember, it will be contagious and it will return to you! As you lift someone up, you too, will be lifted up.

Don't be too hard on yourself either - be kind to yourself, too!

DAY SIXTEEN

Live, Love, Laugh

"Laughter is the shortest distance between two people."
Victor Borge[22]

Laughter is good medicine.

Although I don't find myself funny, my friends assure me that I do really have a sense of humour! What about you? How do you feel about your own sense of humour? What makes you smile and causes you to break out into laughter? Life is tough, but we read in Scripture:

> *A happy heart is good medicine and a cheerful mind works healing, but a broken spirit dries up the bones.*
> *(Proverbs 17:22, AMPC)*

Laughter and joy are good for us. The Lord designed it that way. He not only wants us to enjoy life, but He's actually made it to be good medicine for us.

Determine Your Direction

I have some fabulous friends and those I can be around who do me good. I know that before too long together we will be laughing, sometimes at the most insignificant or absurd things, yet the belly laughs and streaming tears promote such a sense of well-being!

Did you know there are actually a few different types of laughter mentioned in Scripture? It may or may not surprise you when I say that not all of them are good.

There is the laughter of unbelief... Abraham and Sarah were desperate to have a child and the Lord answered their request, but because Sarah had given up all hope she laughed when she heard the news that she was going to have a baby.

(Sarah was listening in the tent door which was behind him.) Now Abraham and Sarah were old, well advanced in age; and Sarah had passed the age of childbearing. Therefore, Sarah laughed within herself, saying, "After I have grown old, shall I have pleasure, my lord being old also?" And the LORD said to Abraham, "Why did Sarah laugh, saying, 'Shall I surely bear a child, since I am old?' Is anything too hard for the LORD? At the appointed time I will return to you, according to the time of life, and Sarah shall have a son." But Sarah denied it, saying, "I did not laugh," for she was afraid. And He said, "No, but you did

laugh!"
(Genesis 18:10-15, NKJV)

There is a mocking laughter. We find an example of this in the event where Jesus went to heal Jairus' daughter. Upon reaching the house where the child lay dead, He assured the onlookers that she was only sleeping. Their unbelief was disparaging.

When He came into the house, He permitted no one to go in except Peter, James, and John, and the father and mother of the girl. Now all wept and mourned for her; but He said, "Do not weep; she is not dead, but sleeping." And they ridiculed Him, knowing that she was dead. But He put them all outside, took her by the hand and called, saying, "Little girl, arise." Then her spirit returned, and she arose immediately.
(Luke 8:51-55)

They laughed him to scorn because of unbelief. It is sad for those who haven't yet trusted in Jesus, their unbelief can release the spirit of mockery.

Do not be deceived, God is not mocked; for whatever a man sows, that he will also reap. For he who sows to his flesh will of the flesh reap corruption, but he who sows to the Spirit will of the Spirit

reap everlasting life.
(Galatians 6:7-8)

The Bible also speaks specifically about the laughter of a fool: *"For as the crackling of thorns under a pot so is the laughter of the fool."* *(Ecclesiastes 7:6)*

Here is the picture of a pot hanging over a crackling fire and when the fire goes out, there is the silence. Barnes' Notes on the Bible describes it to be "Noisy while it lasts, and quickly extinguished."[23] The fool can be laughing one minute, but can plummet into self-consciousness and depression the next.

The fool has said in his heart, "There is no God."
(Psalm 14:1; Psalm 53:1)

This is a true story of a man who lived many years ago. One day he went to his doctor's surgery, that of Dr. James Hamilton of Manchester, England. The man had a skinny grey and sad face. Dr. Hamilton noticed the depressed look on his face and asked, "Are you sick?" His immediate reply was, "Yes doctor, I'm sick with a deadly disease and I'm depressed with life… I can't find anything that makes me laugh. I have nothing to live for. Doctor, can you help me? Unless you help me, I will kill myself! What shall I do?" The Doctor offered his best advice.

Live, Love, Laugh

"You need a change of pace and you need to laugh. Laughter is medicine. Go to the circus tonight and see Grimaldi the clown. Grimaldi is the funniest man alive! I saw him a couple of nights ago and I'm still laughing when I think of him. He will cure you." The man turned in sorrow to the doctor, "Doctor, please don't joke with me, I am Grimaldi!"[24]

It is true that we can be filled with laughter one minute and filled with depression the next. Maybe you are going through or processing tragedy, trauma, grief or pain. Finding the true source of joy and leaning into Jesus will make all the difference between nothing to live for and a destiny to fulfil.

> *For David, after he had served the purpose of God in his own generation, fell asleep, and was laid among his fathers.*
> *(Acts 13:36, ESV)*

May you be one of whom it can be said that you reached your destiny and served God's purposes.

There are two more references to laughter in the Bible I have yet to share with you. There is the laughter of God! Yahweh laughs at his enemies, at those who plot and plan against Him.

Determine Your Direction

Why do the heathens rage and the people imagine a vain thing? The Kings of the Earth set themselves, and the rulers take council together against the LORD and against his anointed, saying 'Let break their bands asunder and cast away their cords from us. He that sitteth in the heavens shall laugh: The LORD shall have them in derision.
(Psalm 2:1-4, KJV)

At the end of the day, the enemies of God will find themselves face to face with Him. Every person laughing now, will be called to give an account before their Maker.

The Lord makes wisdom available to those who will humbly seek it. Wisdom itself has a voice and replies to the scornful, foolish mockers.

"How long, you simple ones, will you love simplicity? For scorners delight in their scorning, and fools hate knowledge. Turn at my rebuke; surely I will pour out my spirit on you; I will make my words known to you. Because I have called and you refused, I have stretched out my hand and no one regarded, because you disdained all my counsel, and would have none of my rebuke, I also will laugh at your calamity; I will mock when your terror comes, when your terror comes like a storm, and your destruction comes like a whirlwind, when distress and anguish come upon you. "Then they

will call on me, but I will not answer; they will seek me diligently, but they will not find me. Because they hated knowledge and did not choose the fear of the LORD, they would have none of my counsel and despised my every rebuke. Therefore, they shall eat the fruit of their own way, and be filled to the full with their own fancies.
(Proverbs 1:22-31, NKJV)

Finally, there is the laughter of Heaven. There is great rejoicing in the presence of the Lord and there is great rejoicing amongst the angels when a sinner repents and turns back to God.

Likewise, I say to you, there is joy in the presence of the angels of God over one sinner who repents."
(Luke 15:10)

To end our topic on laughter, I thought I would share some non-biblical quotes by some well-known public figures:

> "*I will follow up the upward road today.*
> *I will keep my face to the light.*
> *I will think high thoughts as I go my way.*
> *I will do what I know is right.*
> *I will look for the flowers by the side of the road*
> *and I will laugh and love and be strong.*

Determine Your Direction

I will try to lighten another's load this day as I fair along.
Then I will determine to set my face like flint
and I'll determine to laugh and laugh and be strong."
(Mary Edgar, author)

"Those who do not know how to weep with their whole heart,
don't know how to laugh either."
(Golda Meir, fourth Prime Minister of Israel
(March 1969 – June 1974))

"An optimist laughs to forget and a pessimist forgets to laugh."
(Tom Nansbury, author)

"Laughter connects you with people.
It's almost impossible to maintain
any kind of distance or any sense of social hierarchy
when you're just howling with laughter.
Laughter is a force for democracy."
(John Cleese, actor, comedian, screenwriter and producer)

"Laughter has no foreign accent."
(Paul Lowney, author)

Live, Love, Laugh

"Laughter is God's hand on the shoulder of a troubled world."
(Bettenell Huntznicker, public figure)

*"Of all the days the day on which one has not laughed
is the one most surely wasted."*
(Sebastien Roch, actor)

*"We don't laugh because we're happy,
we're happy because we laugh."*
(William James, philosopher)

*"You don't stop laughing because you grow old.
You grow old because you stop laughing."*
(Michael Pritchard, comedian and youth counselor)

*"Your body cannot heal without play
Your mind cannot heal without laughter.
Your soul cannot heal without joy."*
(Catherine Rippenger Fenwick, psychologist)

As you *determine your direction* make sure it includes laughter along the way!

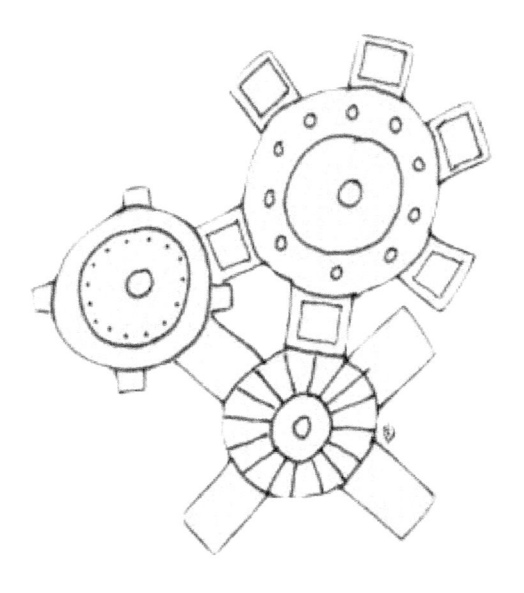

DAY SEVENTEEN

Momentum

Are you a 'Completer-Finisher' or do you have endless unfinished projects and half-read books around? I would like to think I'm a Completer-Finisher. However, in reality I will often start something, or pick up that new book, with all good intentions to make it my single focus, yet more often than not it ends up joining the rest in the 'waiting to be finished' pile.

So… Today, we are going to set our compass right so that we may move along successfully through to completion. Immediately after we start something, we need momentum to help us reach the desired goal. How can we gain, maintain and increase momentum? Obviously, we have to get off the starting block!

Whatever you have set in motion, has to be kept in motion. If you are stationary, not going anywhere, you are going to need something to ignite your first move. This year, I have embarked on writing this book. As a new project for me, the hardest part was firstly committing to the process. I also decided to enrol on two courses. Making the decision to register with these was additionally hard, because that meant payment and payment meant I was *really* committed!

Movement and momentum are based on speed. Isaac Newton's first Law of Motion demonstrated that unless an object at rest was acted upon by a force, it would remain at rest, whereas an object in motion will stay in motion. An obvious notion, but if we apply this law to what we're talking about, it adds another dimension to our thinking: That unless someone - or something - causes change, whatever it is will stay the same. A simple visual, but a powerful one as we ponder on the prospect of forward motion in our lives, being open and willing to change as God wants us to. We never want to stagnate. The glorious promise of God to you is that by His grace and power, you are changing.

> *Now the Lord is the Spirit; and where the Spirit of the Lord is, there is liberty. But we all, with unveiled face, beholding as in a mirror the glory of the Lord, are being transformed into the same image from glory to glory, just as by the Spirit of the Lord.*
> *(2 Corinthians 3:17-18)*

His powerful love also takes us from faith to faith, from strength to strength and from victory to victory.

It takes hope, trust and obedience to keep advancing in our lives. We keep our vision forward, at what lies ahead. We put our hope in God's unfailing Word to us and the promises He has given. We exercise faith in Who He is and we obey His commands, willingly following His invitation to discipleship.

> *Where there is no vision [no redemptive revelation of God], the people perish.*
> *(Proverbs 29:18, AMPC)*

It is so important to have vision and to keep in the forefront of your mind what the Lord has said and revealed to you. We can trust God with what lies beyond, because He is a good Father to us.

Hope helps us to dream. Hope helps us to pursue goals. Hope helps us to aim strategically. Hope gives momentum to our ambitions. Hope is powerful and brings things into manifestation. Hope fuels faith:

> *(Abraham) Who against hope believed in hope, that he might become the father of many nations, according to that which was spoken, So shall thy seed be. And being not weak in faith, he considered not his own body now dead, when he was about an hundred years old, neither yet the deadness of Sarah's womb: he staggered not at the promise of God through unbelief; but was strong in faith, giving glory to God; (Romans 4:18-20, KJV)*

Determine Your Direction

As hope is stirred up in us through unwavering belief, then it is easier to trust and obey.

Imagine a cyclist at the top of a hill. To increase momentum, the cyclist must tilt her weight forward in order to reduce resistance against the wind, so that she will remain balanced and streamlined. Together with pedalling, she has velocity plus mass to provide momentum. Conversely, momentum can be interrupted and stopped. Imagine again the cyclist in motion down that hill. There are two ways of stopping… Either she will apply the brakes, or she'll land in a heap at the bottom!

It is much the same in life. Often people will start something new, from projects to relationships, to ventures and endeavours, with energy and exuberance. Initially it is all exciting, like the buzz and speed the cyclist experiences of the downhill, and can sometimes be intriguing. But unfortunately, more times than most the going starts to get tough. The downhill doesn't last forever; the road levels out, may become bumpy, or may suddenly begin a steep incline. Challenges are presented - the newness pales, the mundane kicks in, the excitement fades and the energy can subside. Here is a key: Learn to keep in the rhythm of life that the Lord sets for you. If you are applying the brakes a little here-and-there during your downhill moments, you won't suddenly lose balance (worse scenario, crash) when you reach the bottom. Jesus knows your pace and wants you to be in alignment with His Spirit.

However, if we do get distracted and suddenly find ourselves in a difficult place, then may we know that

> *Through the LORD's mercies we are not consumed, because His compassions fail not. They are new every morning; great is Your faithfulness.*
> *(Lamentations 3:22-23, NKJV)*

Remember, the Lord's love is *steadfast*. It is resolute and relentless, strong, unwavering and dependable.

Like the Lord's love, be steadfast and passionate in your pursuits keeping a rhythm that is hand-in-hand with Him, so that there may be longevity on your life-road ahead, enabling you to arrive at the right time, and in one piece, at your God-given destination.

You may have guessed that I love to keep things moving! I love to keep things fresh. The essence of life is all about new, fresh, flowing creativity and fullness. Don't self-sabotage by putting your brakes on too suddenly, or crash because you've been going ahead under your own steam. Obedience is the key. Listen to what the Lord wants you to do and walk with Him. He is not in a hurry. Watch out for how much energy you are expending in keeping something moving... This is a good indicator as to whether the Lord is in it. The Spirit gives life and all that He calls you to, *He* will supply the inspiration and power to maintain the momentum!

DAY EIGHTEEN

Nourished to Flourish

Garbage in - garbage out!! Don't eat too much cake .... whoops too late! In my quest to bless a friend on his birthday I made a cake, but then Steve saw me baking and joined me in the kitchen to make his famous flapjack! Whilst the cake was baking in the oven, I came across another great recipe for a walnut tea bread and just because I already had all the ingredients to make it, I went right ahead. On top of this my best friend baked the most delicious mince pies for me to dig in to a day or so later. Now tell me please, how will I ever win the war to lose excess weight? (I had a very big slice of my friend's birthday cake that I had made!) It all was tasty and very enjoyable. But it is debatable as to how nourishing it was.

In order to flourish, grow and develop, we need the good stuff. Then, in uncertain times you will be secure, in the midst of frenetic activity you will remain productive and in an age of hopelessness and aimlessness, you will have direction!

I choose to take vitamins and supplements to boost my immune system, encourage good hair and nail condition and growth, to maintain gut health and joint flexibility and to look after my overall general wellbeing. We should be able to get everything we need from a well-balanced healthy diet, but it helps to get any further assistance that is available. Food nourishment is vital. But what about spiritual nourishment? The writer of Psalm 92 puts it this way…

> *But the godly will flourish like palm trees and grow strong like the cedars of Lebanon. For they are transplanted to the LORD's own house. They flourish in the courts of our God.*
> *(Psalm 92:12-13, NLT)*[25]

Flourish means to break forth as a bud, to spread out, to fly, to be abundant. My desire is that as you journey through this devotional and look to *determine your direction,* you sense how you are budding, flourishing and spreading out.

As plants and trees flourish…

> *Let your roots grow down into him, and let your lives be built on him. Then your faith will grow strong in the truth you were taught, and you will overflow with thankfulness.*
> *(Colossians 2:7, NLT)*

Momentum

If you want to be like a tree planted by water that becomes strong, it can only the roots have to go down deep.

> *But blessed are those who trust in the LORD and have made the LORD their hope and confidence. They are like trees planted along a riverbank, with roots that reach deep into the water. Such trees are not bothered by the heat or worried by long months of drought. Their leaves stay green, and they never stop producing fruit. (Jeremiah 17:7-8, NLT)*

In the New King James version, verse eight has an additional line that reads, "And will not be anxious in the year of drought". Now right there is a strategy for dealing with anxiety and worry! Stay at Jesus' feet. Keep drinking in His presence.

In a hurried and busy generation and culture, we must set aside time for the true nourishment. So many people today feel desperately empty. However, when we are being nourished rightly, we feel fulfilled and complete, like we've had a good meal. There are those living hopelessly and aimlessly through life. When we are nourished, we gain energy and a sense of purpose and direction. The more nourishment we gain, the more godly ambition grows - even overflows. The seeds within us break open to become the fruit of nourishment for others.

Determine Your Direction

Today, you can bud, blossom, break out and flourish. As your aspiration levels rise, allow it to flow out from you and benefit others. May you overflow with peace, success and fruitfulness.

The Lord is our Shepherd and will lead us to where we can receive nourishment (Psalm 23). He also feeds us, fills us and nourishes us Himself. It's not enough just to know God as a Shepherd who leads. For me, I flourish when I know Him as the Shepherd who feeds.

DAY NINETEEN

Seize Every Opportunity

Seize the day!

The morning I wrote today's devotional, I was up particularly early. I rose from my slumber at 4.15am, so I would be in time to attend an international zoom call praying with Christians from around the world, seeking the Lord's heart on the issues of our current climate…

It is important that we seize every opportunity. (Although I must confess to feeling more like the day had seized me rather than I had seized it!) I am of the age and living in the UK when I can remember a television programme called *Opportunity Knocks*. It started out on the radio in 1949 and it appeared on television screens in June 1956. There were various reruns of the programme in 1964, 1979 and 1987 and it was a show where people could exhibit their singing, dancing, comedy, illusion acts (or whatever else.) The audience at home and in-studio would cast their vote for which of these wonderful acts should progress through the stages of the competition, to end up winning a contract leading to celebrity fame and fortune.

Determine Your Direction

Today's versions of *Opportunity Knocks* are the likes of *Britain's Got Talent, America's Got Talent, The Voice,* amongst a growing number of others, through which opportunity is offered to express your gift, talent or expertise.

Opportunity is like a doorway: It opens up and when it is presented, you have to take it or risk it closing.

Opportunity is more often than not a chance meeting. It could be an unscheduled, surprising and unknown moment where the conditions are just right for the occasion.

The Lord gives us opportunities on a daily basis to partner with Heaven and reach out to the world with His blessing and goodness. He wants us to take opportunities to change someone's world. He wants us to seize the moment and influence Earth with Heaven's resources. Through Christ we can redeem time, buying it for His Kingdom purposes.

> *(See then that you walk circumspectly, not as fools but as wise, redeeming the time, because the days are evil. Therefore do not be unwise, but understand what the will of the Lord is.*
> *Ephesians 5:15-17, NKJV)*

Seize Every Opportunity

Time is made up of moments, but it is what you do with them that counts. Are you watching out each day for His opportunities?

> *"Your talent is God's gift to you.*
> *What you do with it is your gift back to God."*
> *Leo Buscaglia*[26]

Today is God's gift to us, but how we use it is our gift back to Him. It is good to reflect at the end of each day, reviewing what you spent most of your time doing and asking yourself where you had an impact, or made a difference. Did you seek to enhance somebody's life and fill up some deficit somewhere, or did you spend the day worrying about things you can't handle, change or control?

> *But seek (aim at and strive after) first of all His kingdom and His righteousness (His way of doing and being right), and then all these things taken together will be given you besides. So do not worry or be anxious about tomorrow, for tomorrow will have worries and anxieties of its own. Sufficient for each day is its own trouble. (Matthew 6:33-34, AMPC)*

We will derive benefits from taking the opportunities that God gives us, but we may not see or experience these results until Heaven! Whatever we do, we should do it with the Kingdom of God in view:

Determine Your Direction

Therefore, whether you eat or drink, or whatever you do, do all to the glory of God.
(1 Corinthians 10:31, NKJV)

Here are some more wonderful Scriptures encouraging and instructing us to keep our gaze on Christ, so that God will get all the glory for the exploits we achieve.

Nor do men light a lamp and put it under a peck measure, but on a lamp stand, and it gives light to all in the house. Let your light so shine before men that they may see your moral excellence and your praiseworthy, noble, and good deeds and recognise and honour and praise and glorify your Father Who is in heaven.
(Matthew 5:15-16, AMPC)

Your lives light up the world. For how can you hide a city that stands on a hilltop? And who would light a lamp and then hide it in an obscure place? Instead, it's placed where everyone in the house can benefit from its light. So don't hide your light! Let it shine brightly before others, so that your commendable works will shine as light upon them, and then they will give their praise to your Father in heaven.
(Matthew 5:14-16, TPT)

Seize Every Opportunity

And let us not lose heart and grow weary and faint in acting nobly and doing right, for in due time and at the appointed season we shall reap, if we do not loosen and relax our courage and faint. So then, as occasion and opportunity open up to us, let us do good [morally] to all people [not only being useful or profitable to them, but also doing what is for their spiritual good and advantage]. Be mindful to be a blessing, especially to those of the household of faith [those who belong to God's family with you, the believers].
(Galatians 6:9-10, AMPC)

Keeping in step with the Holy Spirit, with our conduct controlled by the Holy Spirit, will ensure that our direction in life is being determined by Him.

If we live in the Spirit, let us also walk in the Spirit.
(Galatians 5:25, NKJV)

Take every opportunity today, to make an impact for good. *Determine your direction…* Seize the day and enjoy whatever you put your mind to as you follow the Lord.

DAY TWENTY

Pause, Pray, Purpose

Let's talk about prayer. No matter where you are on your journey, prayer matters. I know there are those who would say they don't really believe that God exists, but they still pray, just in case!

Prayer is like a key in a lock to open not just opportunities on Earth, but supernatural heavenly assistance. God is there and God does hear every lifted voice to him, whether in praise or pain.

> *I am passionately in love with God because he listens to me. He hears my prayers and answers them. As long as I live I'll keep praying to him, for he stoops down to listen to my heart's cry. Death once stared me in the face, and I was close to slipping into its dark shadows. I was terrified and overcome with sorrow. I cried out to the Lord, "God, come and save me!" He was so kind, so gracious to me. Because of his passion toward me, he made everything right and he restored me.*
> *(Psalm 116:1-5, TPT)*

Determine Your Direction

The Lord always does something in response to sincere, heartfelt prayer.

I remember as a teenager, I was looking for truth. I was asking questions about the meaning of life and existence. I simply prayed this, "If you are there God, in Heaven and if you are real then please show Yourself to me. Make Yourself known to me." I actually challenged the Lord to prove it to me. Some might argue that the coincidences that followed were just that, matter-of-fact coincidences. But they really were not. You see, God has a way of uniquely drawing a person to Himself. For me, He showed up in my circumstances and on my behalf, in a way that was undeniable. From that moment, I began a journey into the heart of The Father… In His goodness and graciousness, He has proved Himself to me. He has never let me down, has definitely answered more times than I can recall, and my life feels truly secure in His hands.

To become a person of prayer takes time. That is why today's devotional is about prayer and, as the title states, about the 'pause'. Prayer is the interaction and vehicle of encountering the heart and mind of God - you can simply tell him what is on your heart. You don't need fancy language, or eloquent words. If you wait - He will respond. You will soon find that this is the easiest way to develop a friendship with the Lord. To talk to The Father, to Jesus the Son and the Holy Spirit about everything and anything, being unafraid to ask questions.

He is waiting for you. He wants to share His heart and He wants your partnership in His plans for His world. There can be no greater privilege for a believer than to partner in God's work.

This is where the "Lord's Prayer" becomes reality:

> *In this manner, therefore, pray: Our Father in heaven, hallowed be Your name. Your kingdom come. Your will be done on earth as it is in heaven. Give us this day our daily bread. And forgive us our debts, as we forgive our debtors. And do not lead us into temptation, but deliver us from the evil one. For Yours is the kingdom and the power and the glory forever. Amen.*
> *(Matthew 6:9-13, NKJV)*

You might want to use each phrase as a starting point and take a few minutes pausing on each sentence, to flow with His Spirit as He leads you to pray for His Kingdom advancement today.

DAY TWENTY-ONE

Selah Reflection: Understanding Shabbat Rest

We find reference to the Sabbath in the New Testament.

> *So let no one judge you in food or in drink, or regarding a festival or a new moon or sabbaths, which are a shadow of things to come, but the substance is of Christ.*
> (Colossians 2:16-17)

In other words, don't judge anyone, whether they choose to observe the Sabbath or not. Sabbath rest is being restored to its original covenantal purpose which is to be a blessing from God. There may be times when you have to work on a Sabbath. There is no restriction that states you have to take your rest on a particular day. You won't go to hell if you work on a Sabbath or choose to help someone on the Sabbath. Jesus healed on the Sabbath. He is our example. But there is a blessing to receive by obeying the Word of God to rest. Miss your Sabbath and you miss a blessing. Sabbath is not a time to perform religious acts such as

Determine Your Direction

fasting or by being miserable.

We shouldn't legislate which day to celebrate. Let the Lord schedule your days. The goal is to enjoy spending time with Him. He commanded the Sabbath and here are some reasons why:

1. It is a time to rest from our works and receive His blessings.
2. It is a foreshadowing of what is to come when we rest forever in our eternal dwelling.
3. It is an act of worship, by it we acknowledge The Lord as Creator.
4. It is a picture of salvation.
5. It is designed to restore us and strengthen us.
6. It is an opportunity to trust the Lord for His provision and supply.

Today is about reviewing what you have read since our last *Selah Reflection* on Day Fourteen and evaluating how you can make it work in your life. Here are some topics I have picked from these days, to encourage you.

1. Choose an act of kindness that you can bless someone with today or in the coming week. We can be deceived into believing that "it's the thought that counts." In this case, let's go beyond thinking kind thoughts towards someone and actually reach out and demonstrate it!

Selah Reflection: Understanding Shabbat Rest

2. Ask yourself, in what ways are you flourishing. Really bearing fruit? If you are having difficulty, then ask someone close to you to help you answer this question. Someone who will notice how you are changing and flourishing, as you nourish yourself in the Word and Spirit.

3. Praise the Lord for this pause to reflect on the last six days.

4. Use the rhythm of the Lord's Prayer to inspire you to pray in a different way. Take a sentence and pause… Let Holy Spirit lead you as you pray through it. As you partner with Him, may you experience a surprise encounter of His love pouring through you, as He shares His burdens and heart.

DAY TWENTY-TWO

Question Time

We live in such an incredible age of information and technology. We are bombarded with information coming at us from all sides. Our mobile phones have become TV screens, pushing notifications and news headlines before us whether we like it or not. Of course, the setting control allows the individual to have the final say on what comes through, but often, one has to trawl through piles of unwanted junk mail to finally decide what to keep or unsubscribe from. Going paperless seemed like a great idea, but digital information can be far more overwhelming to deal with, especially for the elderly. (Or digitally challenged!)

As we have learnt, knowledge is increasing rapidly. There are forums galore to give you information on absolutely anything and everything. This is the period we live in. On one hand, the technology and available resources are helpful, but they are easily used in the wrong way and can, if abused, be very harmful and damaging. Let us take a moment to consider your phone and technology usage. How readily do you respond to the demand of the 'ping'? Does your phone rule you, or do you rule your phone? How about emails? Do you feel the daily pressure of having to be tied to your desk?

It may be that you need to allow your mobile to be on silent a little more often, or create an Auto Responder to emails saying something like, "Thank you for your email - I will get back to you just as soon as I can."

I have a friend that always wants the answer to seemingly unanswerable questions. My assurance when I tell her that we do not always need to know, (or that we may never know), does not always satisfy. It is a fact that many questions in life are and will remain unanswered. (Phew! That takes some pressure off already!)

However, it is absolutely okay to ask God questions. The Lord is a communicating God. The clue is in the fact that He has made us with the ability to communicate one to another. We see no more clearly His heart to communicate with us, than in the sending of His Son. He *longs* to communicate with us. He does not want to just hear our shopping list of needs. Neither does He expect us to be waiting passively upon His next directive. We are not robotic in our relationship towards Him. The Lord wants us to seek Him and has designed us with a questioning urge; that longing of heart that to be in pursuit of answers.

We can take encouragement from King David. David was the shepherd

Question Time

boy that went before Saul's vast army against the Philistines, killing the giant called Goliath (see 1 Samuel 16-17).

When David became king, he never presumed to do things a certain way, even when leading a vast army out to war. He went to ask God for direction. Here are some occasions where David inquired of the Lord, for you to study: *1 Samuel 23:2, 1 Samuel 23:4, 1 Samuel 30:8, 2 Samuel 2:1, 2 Samuel 5:19, 2 Samuel 5:23*

David went before God with a humble heart, with his sincere questions, and God responded. He led David into success and favour and He wants to do the same for you and me.

Do you have any questions to ask the Lord? Are you stuck? Are you undecided? Do you need direction? It is OK to ask the question!

Jesus also instructs us to "ask and it shall be given, seek and you will find, knock and the door will be open to you" (Luke 11:9-10).

Take courage in your questioning - God has it covered. He is a big God and has all the answers!

DAY TWENTY-THREE

Reach Out for Revelation

Wisdom and revelation are available to you!

To *determine your direction* in the right way, means making sound choices. It means we have found the way for wisdom to flow to us and out through us. It is important to develop a heart filled with wisdom.

> *So, teach us to number our days, that we may **gain** a heart of wisdom.*
> *(Psalm 90:12, NKJV)*

The *New American Standard* translation writes it this way:

> *So teach us to number our days, that we may **present** to You a heart of wisdom*
> *(Psalm 90:12, NASB)*

The word ***gain*** indicates the acquiring for one's own purpose or advantage whereas the word ***present*** suggests an offering of our hearts towards the Lord. I prefer the NASB in this instance.

Operating with wisdom is knowing the right thing to say and do. However, the application comes with *seeing* the solution. That is why revelation, (the seeing part), is often coupled with wisdom, (the *knowing what to do* part).

> *After these things I looked, and behold, a door standing open in heaven. And the first voice which I heard was like a trumpet speaking with me, saying, "Come up here, and I will show you things which must take place after this." Immediately I was in the Spirit; and behold, a throne set in heaven, and One sat on the throne. And He who sat there was like a jasper and a sardius stone in appearance; and there was a rainbow around the throne, in appearance like an emerald.*
> *(Revelation 4:1-3, NKJV)*

The beloved Apostle John wrote the passage we've just read when, in his final days, he was called "up" into a heavenly realm and shown supernatural visions.

When Jesus was about to return to Heaven, He said to His disciples:

> *However, I am telling you nothing but the truth when I say it is*

profitable (good, expedient, advantageous) for you that I go away. Because if I do not go away, the Comforter (Counsellor, Helper, Advocate, Intercessor, Strengthener, Standby) will not come to you [into close fellowship with you]; but if I go away, I will send Him to you [to be in close fellowship with you].
(John 16:7, AMPC)

But when He, the Spirit of Truth (the Truth-giving Spirit) comes, He will guide you into all the Truth (the whole, full Truth). For He will not speak His own message [on His own authority]; but He will tell whatever He hears [from the Father; He will give the message that has been given to Him], and He will announce and declare to you the things that are to come [that will happen in the future]. He will honour and glorify Me, because He will take of (receive, draw upon) what is Mine and will **reveal (declare, disclose, transmit)** *it to you. Everything that the Father has is Mine. That is what I meant when I said that He [the Spirit] will take the things that are Mine and will* **reveal (declare, disclose, transmit)** *it to you.*
(John 16:13-15, AMPC)

The Holy Spirit is our everyday *Revelator*. His role and ministry to us is to reveal the heart of The Father, the will of The Father, the mind of Christ, things to come and the purposes behind the things that are going on now. He desires to release wisdom, revelation and the secrets of His heart to His people.

> *Surely the Lord GOD does nothing, unless He reveals His secret to His servants the prophets. A lion has roared! Who will not fear? The Lord GOD has spoken! Who can but prophesy?*
> *(Amos 3:7-8, NKJV)*

The purpose of the release of wisdom and revelation is the advancement of God's Kingdom, for His will alone.

> *Therefore I also, after I heard of your faith in the Lord Jesus and your love for all the saints, do not cease to give thanks for you, making mention of you in my prayers: that the God of our Lord Jesus Christ, the Father of glory, may give to you the spirit of wisdom and revelation in the knowledge of Him, the eyes of your understanding being enlightened; that you may know what is the hope of His calling, what are the riches of the glory of His inheritance in the saints, and what is the exceeding greatness of His power toward us who believe, according to the working of His mighty power which He worked in Christ when He raised Him from the dead and seated Him at His right hand in the heavenly places, far above all principality and power and might and dominion, and every name that is named, not only in this age but also in that which*

is to come. And He put all things under His feet, and gave Him to be head over all things to the church, which is His body, the fullness of Him who fills all in all.
(Ephesians 1:15-23)

Revelation is making known something that has previously been unknown. Wisdom is the quality of having experience, knowledge and good judgment that develops as we inquire of the Lord and practice listening. Over time, our ear becomes more attuned to hearing Wisdom's voice. As you seek to align yourself with the will of God, ask the Spirit of Wisdom to help you in the decisions you make as you *determine your direction.*

Say this prayer with me: **Lord God, open my eyes to see the hope that lies before me. I choose today to yield my heart to Wisdom's voice for your glory and kingdom advancement, amen.**

DAY TWENTY-FOUR

Strategy

As you think about where you are going, be strategic and plan well.

It's not always easy to stay on course… You need to ask Holy Spirit for a plan and strategy to outwit opposing forces that will try to hinder you from fulfilling your purpose destiny.

To plan is simply to think ahead; a route from 'A-to-B' thought about and decided upon in advance. Once you have received your directive from Holy Spirit, the Word of God tells us to put on His armour to further protect us from the opposing forces of darkness:

> *Finally, my brethren, be strong in the Lord and in the power of His might. Put on the whole armour of God, that you may be able to stand against the wiles of the devil. For we do not wrestle against flesh and blood, but against principalities, against powers, against the rulers of the darkness of this age, against spiritual hosts of wickedness in the heavenly places. Therefore, take up the whole armour of God, that you may be able to*

Determine Your Direction

withstand in the evil day, and having done all, to stand. (Ephesians 6:10-11)

Here is the key strategy. Taking action by applying the armour of God in preparation for, and assurance of, victory over the wiles of the devil.

As believers, we know we face opposition and it can come in all kinds of ways. If we turn to the Lord like King David and hearken our ear to His voice, we will receive detailed instructions of a plan to outwit and overcome, every time. As Christians, what are we facing? An enemy who prowls around, tells lies, tricks people with his deceptive ways, and goes on to torment and destroy lives. All the intentions of the dark rulers are summed up in this passage of Ephesians as **wiles** *of the devil*.

The Greek word for *wiles* is *methodeia and it* means 'cunning arts', 'deceit', 'craft', 'trickery'. You get the picture. Not surprisingly we get our words *method* and *methodical* from this. (Although, most of us will not be aware of its root meaning!) The Word of God makes it very clear that the devil has a strategic *methodical* plan to attempt to destroy each of us.

If we don't have revelation and knowledge, or full assurance of what Jesus has done, we may find ourselves quivering at the thought of spiritual warfare or worse still, we are more likely to fall captive to the distractive tactics and diversions of the enemy. But when we know the rules in this game - that Jesus has already defeated him and taken captive sin, sickness and death - we can rise up and outwit the devil every time!

The word 'strategy' is often associated within military planning and directing. The Oxford dictionary online defines 'strategy' as "a plan of action or policy designed to achieve a major or overall aim"[27] and as "the art or science of planning an overall military operation."

As you determine your direction, include strategy. Together with the Spirits of Wisdom and Revelation, you are on the way to your next level!

DAY TWENTY-FIVE

Thankfulness

Developing a thankful heart and making it a part of your lifestyle, a daily habit, is an important key to staying healthy and happy. Be thankful, be healthy, be happy!

There are workshops, resources, and initiatives that promote gratitude. In today's culture and society there are social and community breakdowns, soaring crime rates and anti-social behaviour. Research shows that raising the awareness of the benefits of gratitude, causes a shift. It is like the glue that holds relationships together. Expressing gratitude has shown to change relationships, communities and organisations, for the better.

An attitude and demonstration of gratitude actually does something positive inside of us. Thanksgiving leads us into joy and rejoicing.

> *Rejoice always, pray without ceasing, in everything give thanks; for this is the will of God in Christ Jesus for you.*
> *(1 Thessalonians 5:18)*

Determine Your Direction

We give thanks *in* everything, not necessarily *for* everything. Here is where some people get duped by the enemy. It seems inconceivable to rejoice and give thanks in tragic and difficult circumstances, but we are instructed to give thanks, despite what is going on. It is all about focus. If we have our focus and thanksgiving directed rightly, it means that The Lord can intervene on our behalf and cause all things to be used for His glory and purpose.

> *And we know that all things work together for good to those who love God, to those who are the called according to His purpose. (Romans 8:28)*

As we make this a part of our lifestyle, it becomes second nature - our natural response. This may surprise you to know that giving thanks is what we are made for and will be an eternal occupation for us, too. It goes on in Heaven right now:

> *Whenever the living creatures give glory and honour and* **thanks** *to Him who sits on the throne, who lives forever and ever, the twenty-four elders fall down before Him who sits on the throne and worship Him who lives forever and ever, and cast their crowns before the throne, saying: "You are worthy, O Lord, to receive glory and honour and power; for You created all things,*

and by Your will they exist and were created."
(Revelation 4:9-11)

Revelation chapter seven confirms how people from all nations, tribes and tongues will be engaged in expressing thankfulness to our God and Saviour Jesus Christ, when we stand before Him:

*After these things I looked, and behold, a great multitude which no one could number, of all nations, tribes, peoples, and tongues, standing before the throne and before the Lamb, clothed with white robes, with palm branches in their hands, and crying out with a loud voice, saying, "Salvation belongs to our God who sits on the throne, and to the Lamb!" All the angels stood around the throne and the elders and the four living creatures, and fell on their faces before the throne and worshiped God, saying: "Amen! Blessing and glory and wisdom, **thanksgiving** and honour and power and might, be to our God forever and ever. Amen."*
(Revelation 7:9-12)

Expressing a sacrifice of thanksgiving does not mean in a begrudging, reluctant or disapproving attitude. No! It means giving of our best! It is our choicest and highest pleasure. However, it becomes even more of a sacrificial offering when we give Him thanks amidst difficult circumstances.

Determine Your Direction

King David needed a place to build an altar to the Lord for his sacrifice, so he purchased the threshing floor from the Jebusite named Arunah. The threshing floor was a place of separation and revelation, where the harvest was prepared by separating the grain from the straw. In this way, they would collect the best part of the crop. Significantly, David would not take it, rather he paid for it:

> *Then the king said to Araunah, "No, but I will surely buy it from you for a price;* **nor will I offer burnt offerings to the LORD my God with that which costs me nothing.**" *So David bought the threshing floor and the oxen for fifty shekels of silver. And David built there an altar to the LORD, and offered burnt offerings and peace offerings. So the LORD heeded the prayers for the land, and the plague was withdrawn from Israel.*
> *(2 Samuel 24:24-25)*

This is a great example of how we should be. May the sacrifices from our heart be acceptable to the Lord in every way.

> *You have loosed my bonds. I will offer to You the sacrifice of thanksgiving, And will call upon the name of the LORD.*
> *(Psalm 116:16-17)*

> *But I will sacrifice to You with the voice of thanksgiving; I will pay*

Thankfulness

what I have vowed. Salvation is of the LORD."
(Jonah 2:9)

Therefore by Him let us continually offer the sacrifice of praise to God, that is, the fruit of our lips, giving thanks to His name. But do not forget to do good and to share, for with such sacrifices God is well pleased.
(Hebrews 13:15-16)

Begin to just take a few minutes extra each day, starting today, to give thanks to God for something that you haven't been thankful for. Ordinary everyday things, which perhaps you take for granted. Pause and take a moment to think. Let your heart overflow with gratitude, for all things.

DAY TWENTY-SIX

Unique

You may at some time have been the recipient of a duplicate birthday card. Even though the printed outside looks the same, each card is unique with the sentiments and greetings within.

It is the fond greeting, word of appreciation or a specific Scripture that makes it different to the next and makes it unique. Steve bought me a single freshwater pearl on a gold necklace to celebrate our wedding. Unfortunately, it was stolen from our home…but I remember it vividly, because it was so distinctive. When we went to the same jeweller to replace it, we were told that each pearl is unique and therefore irreplaceable.

Scientists assure us that not one blade of grass is exactly the same as the next. Similarly with snowflakes - each is uniquely different in pattern and design. This can be proven with incredible magnification. What a Creator! That He should go to such extents to make each snowflake so individual! So… What about each one of His children? There may be similarities here and there, but never a carbon copy.

Determine Your Direction

I happened across a TV programme recently where there was a young man whose natural appearance resembled the celebrity singer/songwriter Ed Sheeran. Ed is a well-known, well sought-after celebrity. It became apparent that the look-alike was hired by a company to see if they could pass him off in exclusive events and gatherings! He was flown right across the globe and managed easy entrance to an enormous concert as a VIP, because everyone thought he actually was Ed Sheeran! The TV programme was entertaining to say the least! The producers of the show went on to introduce several other young men who also looked like Ed Sheeran, as well as the real Ed Sheeran himself. They discussed how easy it was to pass for another *until* one of them was asked a question that only the real Ed was expected to know the answer to.

You are special and unique! You are not to be compared to another and neither should we compare ourselves with others. Comparison can be self-destructive for it can lead to feelings of not being good enough. It can lead also to jealousy and resentfulness. If we quit comparing ourselves then it gives us more space to blossom and grow in our character and gifts. So today, don't allow comparison to bind you and stop your forward momentum.

I reiterate: You are totally unique and therefore irreplaceable and as such, carry a high value in God's sight.

Unique

For I know the thoughts that I think toward you, says the LORD, thoughts of peace and not of evil, to give you a future and a hope. Then you will call upon Me and go and pray to Me, and I will listen to you. And you will seek Me and find Me, when you search for Me with all your heart. I will be found by you, says the LORD, and I will bring you back from your captivity.
(Jeremiah 29:11-14a)

The Lord endearingly said this through the prophet Jeremiah to the Children of Israel. However as with every word in the Bible, we can apply it personally. The Lord has good plans for you as you *determine your direction,* as long as you keep your hand is in His. Jesus, your good shepherd, is going to make sure that you have unique and special experiences along the way, intrinsically designed just for you.

You are not like anyone else! Today, hold your head up high and enjoy being you.

DAY TWENTY-SEVEN

Vision in the Valleys

The road ahead isn't always straight, the path is not always smooth - there are hills, mountains and valleys. Everyone goes through a valley at some point. The good news is, you can still know victory in the valley and as you stay forward focused, your vision will encourage and inspire you to keep pressing onwards.

What does victory mean? Victory is the overcoming of an enemy; to endeavour against all odds or difficulties. What are you facing today that you need to have victory in? What circumstances surround you that you need to triumph over?

I was listening to someone recently talking about dreams. Dreams that need to be reawakened. I don't mean the dreams that we have when we sleep, but the dreams that are our hopes and vision for the future.

We all have desires and aspirations, things our heart yearns for that lies beyond our present reality. Vision is necessary for motivating and creating incentive and stimulus to move forward. The gift of ambition creates energy, strength, and stamina to go to great lengths that under normal circumstances would not be there.

Do you have a picture of your future? Do you have vision? Do you have any ambition or desire to be living differently to how you are now? We must realise that we are living today in yesterday's tomorrow. In other words, the choices we made in our yesterdays have framed and fashioned the day we are enjoying - or enduring - today. Therefore, if you want a greater tomorrow you have to set your different course **today**. You can *determine your direction today* so that the vision for your future can become clearer. If you can see it, you can have it. If you can see it, you can go there; and if you can see it, you can create it. Vision is very, very important if we are to take action to change our life and the world for others.

After Walt Disney died, people discussed the wonderful family amusement parks he created. Someone said, "I wish Disney could have seen this…" Someone who had lived close by him and who knew him simply replied, "he did."

"All our dreams can come true,
if we have the courage to pursue them."
Walt Disney[28]

Visions in the Valleys

Sometimes when we go through 'the valley', all hope seems to be dashed and we can almost give up. At those times we need to be encouraged that the valley still plays an important role in helping us grow into our potential. We can adopt the attitude to push through to victory, because of the greater One, Jesus Christ, who lives in every believer.

Jesus has promised He is with us as we walk through valley and will never leave us. Because of this, we are never alone, even in our darkest times. We can raise up our heads to the heavens and declare, "I look up to the mountains - does my help come from there? My help comes from the LORD, who made heaven and earth!" (Psalm 121:1-2, NLT) We can ask the Spirit of Jesus to give us sight for what lies beyond and give us the courage to declare it. By His strength we can live beyond our present boundaries, because the Lord is our Shepherd and in Him, we *shall not want*.
(Psalm 23)

Declare today: *I can walk through the valleys, gaining vision and realising potential. I am an overcomer and more than a conqueror, because of Christ Jesus Who died for me. I am made for victory!*

You are a victor not a victim and you can walk through any valley if you hold tight to the Lord's hand and your eye on the path ahead. Ask the Lord to clarify for you the place where He wants you to be in the months ahead. There is one sure thing - it will be a good place.

DAY TWENTY-EIGHT

Selah Reflection: Understanding Shabbat Rest

And He (Jesus) said to them, The Sabbath was made for man, and not man for the Sabbath. Therefore, the Son of Man is also Lord of the Sabbath.
(Mark 2:27-28, NKJV)

Let Jesus show you how to rest and enjoy your day today. He is Lord of the Sabbath.

You have six days each week for your ordinary work, but the seventh day is a Sabbath day of complete rest, an official day for holy assembly. It is the LORD's Sabbath day, and it must be observed wherever you live.
(Leviticus 23:3, NLT)

The Scripture instructs us to do no regular work. There is no religious protocol to follow. The goal is to enjoy God and His blessings. It is a

Determine Your Direction

time to be nourished and refreshed.

It is rest for our bodies, but it also has a spiritual benefit. We can find an abiding place of faith where we experience and encounter the Lord in a deep way. Relationship and revelation take time. Sabbath is a place of rest and an abiding position, to encourage the deepening of our relationship with Him.

During your day of rest today, why don't you consider:

1. Asking the Lord three questions that you would like Him to answer. Write them down in your journal. As you ask, wait and worship.

2. Maybe consider whether you could ask the question in a different way? Lean in to the Lord and wait for His Word. Wait in His Presence and write down any particular Scriptures Holy Spirit reminds you of with relation to your question.

3. Pray in the Spirit. Wait and look to see what He is saying. Write down any immediate answer. If your question remains unanswered, stay open, wait and watch - the answer may come in a way and at a time you do not expect. The Lord

Selah Reflection: Understanding Shabbat Rest

does not answer immediately, but if your heart remains open to hear, at the right moment the answer will be released to you.

4. As you ponder on the topics of the last six days, think about receiving revelation. How do *you* receive from the Lord? As each of us is unique, so He will speak to you uniquely. Some ways God speaks is through words, pictures, discernment, night-dreams, day-dreams, visions, through our physical senses as well as our spiritual ones.

5. Take time to wait in the Lord's Presence today and ask Him to speak to you about any of the topics you have read about so far. Worship and if you have received the Spirit's gift of tongues, spend time praying in it. Then quieten yourself for a few moments… Write down in your journal what you hear or sense the Lord saying to you

6. Ask the Lord to tell you how He sees you and what He would say to you *about* you! As you record in your journal, write as if the Lord Himself is penning a letter to you. Open with a salutation that is personal, for example "My beloved daughter," or "My beloved son".

Determine Your Direction

Let the light of His truth - *The Truth* - flow in you and bring you healing today, as Jesus Himself lifts up your head.

DAY TWENTY-NINE

Wise Words Win

Be a blessing with the words you choose!!

Words create and frame our future. Choose wise words to win! You can build, bless and encourage others with what you choose to roll off your tongue. You can make a difference with the words you choose to speak. I think the way that God has designed communication is fascinating and in particular the way that the Hebrew language has been preserved. It's very interesting and worth researching out. Allow me to share with you a little about this intriguing language.

Each letter in the Hebrew alphabet (or aleph-bet) has a numerical value. The first ten letters have the values one to ten. The next nine letters are valued twenty, thirty...up to one-hundred. The remainder are valued two-hundred, three-hundred and four-hundred.

The Hebraic alphabet is intrinsically linked to the calendar dates and God's 'Appointed Times', which we discover in Scripture. In addition, each number in Hebrew has a corresponding symbol and as prophetic people, we can interpret what the Lord is saying by looking at the meanings behind the symbols, words, letters and numbers.

According to the Hebraic calendar, the decade we have just entered (2020, which in the Hebraic calendar is 5780) is the **Pey** decade. In Hebrew, the number eighty is *pey* and it means 'mouth'.

The previous decade corresponding to seventy contained the word *Ayin* running throughout. *Ayin* means '*sight*', '*eyes*', '*to look*'. So according to the biblical calendar, we have transitioned from a season of prophetically "seeing", into a season of "declaring, proclaiming and decreeing."

It is very, very important how we use our voice and what we speak out. We frame our future by the words we utter.

Do you recall the statement in Day Twenty-Four, *Vision in the Valleys* where it says "we are living today in yesterday's tomorrow"? The future is dependent on seeing it...and *speaking* it.

Thinking about what you want to accomplish and what you need to achieve is a step in the right direction, but only goes so far towards making it happen. Adversely, thinking and speaking negatively will achieve little and complaining and moaning could actually reverse any good intentions. Worse still, pronouncing words of doom and gloom can activate a curse to bring about failure.

> *Death and life are in the power of the tongue, and those who love it will eat its fruit.*
> *(Proverbs 18:21, NKJV)*

Words are in themselves creative. They are birthed in the nature of God! Words can heal, they can mend and repair, they can build, they can form, they can provide, they can develop, they can unlock, they can publish, they can produce. For God's Words to be activated in your life, you are going to have to put some effort into it. You are going to need to be intentional about speaking words that birth life.

If we speak rightly, we promote healing and wholeness over ourselves and for those in our company.

> *A word fitly spoken is like apples of gold in settings of silver.*
> *(Proverbs 25:11)*

If this challenges you and Holy Spirit is reminding - or even convicting you of words you have said that you shouldn't have - rejoice and raise a hallelujah. It's turnaround time! Repent, receive forgiveness and cleansing. Then, the way you turn it around is by declaring into the atmosphere the *opposite* - words of blessing and favour. The Lord will take up those words and cause them to reach the target.

According to research, children need to hear thousands more positive words to counteract the negative ones. The good news is, there are so many promises in God's word that we can never run out of excellent things to meditate on and speak out.

Today, search up Scriptures that declare God's Words of blessing and favour over your life and personalise them as you speak them out. I've written some below to get you started (adapted from John Eckhardt, *Prayers that Activate Blessings* (2011))[29]:

Dear Yahweh, bless me and surround me with favour like a shield
(Psalm 5:12)

Lord, I declare my set time of favour has come
(Psalm 102:13)

Let me have favour with you, Lord, and with men
(1 Samuel 2:26)

I have found wisdom; I have found life and I obtain Your favour
(Proverbs 8:35)

Wise Words Win

Lord, I receive Your blessing for my transgression is forgiven and my sin is covered
(Psalm 32:1)

I receive and walk in the authority of the Kingdom
(Luke 9:1)

DAY THIRTY

Extend, Expand, Enlarge

Can it get any better? When we consider that God's plans for our lives are good, then often that means bigger and better than the here and now. In Matthew chapter seven, Jesus said,

> *Enter by the narrow gate; for wide is the gate and broad is the way that leads to destruction, and there are many who go in by it. Because narrow is the gate and difficult is the way which leads to life, and there are few who find it.*
> *(Matthew 7:13-14)*

The road leading to destruction is broad and the path leading to righteousness is narrow. This is describing the attitudes and desires of the heart which lead us either towards or away from God's purposes for us… The Kingdom of God must always be our priority and seeking it above all else ensures that we receive ***all these things added:***

> *But seek first the Kingdom of God and His righteousness, and all these things shall be added to you. (Matthew 6:33)*

Determine Your Direction

God does not expect His children to live as if fearful of falling from a tight rope, constantly apprehensive of making a mistake; with choices to make, yet paralysed for fear of taking the wrong course. Scripture is very clear about what is right and wrong regarding sin, but there is a life to be lived and enjoyed as unto the Lord that is full and free. Jesus called it "abundant life" (John 10:10).

> *...since the day we heard it, we do not cease to pray for you, and to ask that you may be filled with the knowledge of His will in all wisdom and spiritual understanding; that you may walk worthy of the Lord, fully pleasing Him, being fruitful in every good work and increasing in the knowledge of God; strengthened with all might, according to His glorious power.*
> *(Colossians 1:9-11)*

The Lord wants to expand your horizon and enlarge your territory. Even if there are times where the road seems narrow, the purpose will always be to bring you out and through to somewhere more far reaching, greater standing and fruitfulness.

> *Now Jabez was more honourable than his brothers, and his mother called his name Jabez, saying, "Because I bore him in pain." And Jabez called on the God of Israel saying, "Oh, that You would bless me indeed, and enlarge my territory, that Your hand*

Extend, Expand, Enlarge

would be with me, and that You would keep me from evil, that I may not cause pain!" So God granted him what he requested.
(1 Chronicles 4:9-10)

What an unfortunate start for Jabez, named so because of the pain his mother endured in his birth. Every time his name was spoken, it was a declaration and announcement over and over that he was a pain. This was a negative beginning and it continued throughout his life. However, he turned to the Lord for help and deliverance. He wanted freedom from the restriction and curse that was upon him.

The Lord had not pronounced his name, but he heard his cry and answered him.

There is a word for you today on this that the Lord wants you to know. Your vision and your territory ahead is larger than it is now. Why not pray as Jabez prayed? It is time to extend, expand and enlarge your horizon.

You are born for greatness at such a time as this! That is how you are wired. There is a longing in every person for greatness - not greatness that elevates self in order to make a name for ourselves, but greatness that enables us to make a lasting impact on the world that we live in. As you determine your direction with Jesus at the helm, think big. As you

Determine Your Direction

look towards your goal, your destination, think broader, higher, wider and greater in every way. Remember, Jesus came to give you abundant life - not shallow or dull - but full to overflowing, with his love, joy and peace. Let the overflow commence!

Let the joy and goodness of Christ flow through you, as you anticipate expanding your borders and your territory today.

DAY THIRTY-ONE

Yes & Amen

Prophecies, words, declarations and decrees are *promises*. When God says it, you can believe to see it come to pass. All His promises are 'yes and amen'! In dreaming big, declaring boldly and believing fervently, you will enjoy the fruit as He brings His Word to fulfilment in your life.

I have a printed list of the top one-hundred prophecies recorded in the Old Testament, of the coming Saviour, all of which were that were fulfilled by Jesus of Nazareth. These were spoken some several hundred years before He came to earth and they were fulfilled to the letter.

They are referred to as prophecies because they were declarations. However, we could also call them *promises,* because a promise is something that you look forward to; something you are hopeful for. For those witnessing the prophets speak at that time, I am sure they were anticipating the fulfilment of their words within in their own lifetime. Yet they all died before the coming of the promised Saviour came to pass.

Determine Your Direction

When the time for fulfilment did come, Jesus arriving on the scene was good news. He came to set the captives free, to heal the sick, to deliver the oppressed. He died on the cross to set us free from all the power of the enemy towards us to kill, steal and destroy our life.

The foretelling of the Messiah came to pass in Jesus. You can be certain that the prophecies yet to be fulfilled in Scripture will also come to fruition, including our blessed assurance outlined in first John,

> *And this is the promise that He has promised us—eternal life.*
> *(1 John 2:25)*

Eternal life actually begins right here - the moment we receive salvation. It is a promise that carries us to the end of the age, (or our old age), and beyond.

> *Let us hold fast the confession of our hope without wavering, for He who promised is faithful.*
> *(Hebrews 10:23)*

God will keep his promises.

> *Whose voice then shook the earth; but now He has promised, saying, "Yet once more I shake not only the earth, but also heaven."*

Extend, Expand, Enlarge

> *Now this, "Yet once more," indicates the removal of those things that are being shaken, as of things that are made, that the things which cannot be shaken may remain. Therefore, since we are receiving a kingdom which cannot be shaken, let us have grace, by which we may serve God acceptably with reverence and godly fear. For our God is a consuming fire.*
> *(Hebrews 12:26-29)*

We find such covenants scattered all throughout Scripture. If you have received specific Words from God, He is faithful, no matter what your circumstances say. Hold fast and keep believing - He will complete what He has started.

> *For all the promises of God in Him are Yes, and in Him Amen, to the glory of God through us.*
> *(2 Corinthians 1:20)*

I want to say 'yes and amen' to every promise of God! "Yes I believe" and "Amen, I receive!" How about you?

May you choose to agree, to take gold of and live in the goodness of His promises today. Invest your faith in His Words and like Abraham - don't let them go until you see them fulfilled.

And not being weak in faith, he (Abraham) did not consider his own body, already dead (since he was about a hundred years old), and the deadness of Sarah's womb. He did not waver at the promise of God through unbelief, but was strengthened in faith, giving glory to God, and being fully convinced that what He had promised He was also able to perform. And therefore "it was accounted to him for righteousness."
(Romans 4:19-22)

Take hold of God's promises today and let your faith be ignited, energised and strengthened.

Declare: **"I believe it and I will see it."** Plant God's vow in your heart and let it come forth from your lips. Declare out loud, "the promises of God for me in Christ Jesus are 'yes and Amen'!"

DAY THIRTY-TWO

Zeal

Jesus was fully committed to His purpose and objective. I am so very grateful He was. He was *all in* and so should we be, too.

> *Pilate therefore said to Him, "Are You a king then?" Jesus answered, "You say rightly that I am a king. **For this cause I was born**, and for this cause I have come into the world, that I should bear witness to the truth. Everyone who is of the truth hears My voice."*
> *(John 18:37)*

> *He who sins is of the devil, for the devil has sinned from the beginning. For this purpose, the Son of God was manifested, that He might destroy the works of the devil.*
> *(1 John 3:8)*

Being *all in* is costly. It was costly for Jesus - He gave His all for us through His life, death and resurrection! It demands focus, intention, commitment and follow-through. The foundation that provides this momentum is passion. How passionate for God and His Kingdom are you? How could you describe or measure it? In what ways could your passion increase?

Passion Wins over Mediocrity

The Lord wanted 'a people' whom others, even other nations, could look to for leadership and direction. He wanted His Chosen People (Israel) to stand out as a representative and reflection of Himself. He was never at a stretch to bless and favour them, just like He isn't for us today. Their responsibility - as is ours - was to obey, to follow and to continually seek and desire God above all else. As we read from the accounts in the Old Testament, the people of Israel failed to love and honour Yahweh time and time again, but never did His heart towards them change. So, it is with us.

Passion expresses itself in enthusiasm, intensity and **zeal.** The opposite of which is passivity, apathy and lukewarmness. Jesus had a strong word to the Church in Laodicea about this attitude and lifestyle;

> *So then, because you are lukewarm, and neither cold nor hot, I will vomit you out of My mouth.*
> *(Revelation 3:16)*

Extend, Expand, Enlarge

You will not successfully *determine your direction* in life without commitment, passion and to some degree, **zeal.** Zeal is consuming, like jealousy. It can prompt us to action against something. We gain a glimpse of this through the words of the Psalmist here,

> *Righteous are You, O LORD, and upright are Your judgments. Your testimonies, which You have commanded, are righteous and very faithful. My zeal has consumed me,* ***because my enemies have forgotten Your words.*** *Your word is very pure; therefore Your servant loves it.*
> *(Psalm 119:137-140)*

In Isaiah we read of the zeal of Yahweh Himself:

> *Of the increase of His government and peace there will be no end, upon the throne of David and over His kingdom, to order it and establish it with judgment and justice from that time forward, even forever. The zeal of the LORD of hosts will perform this.*
> *(Isaiah 9:7)*

Zeal can rise up within to the point of overflowing so that others can see and be moved by it.

> *Then he (Jehu) said, "Come with me, and see my zeal for the*

LORD."
(2 Kings 10:16)

It is a powerful inclination and response…

Because zeal for Your house has eaten me up.
(Psalm 69:9)

The Lord Himself is a *jealous* God and also a *zealous* God.

The LORD shall go forth like a mighty man; He shall stir up His zeal like a man of war. He shall cry out, yes, shout aloud; He shall prevail against His enemies.
(Isaiah 42:13)

Again, the word of the LORD of hosts came, saying, "Thus says the LORD of hosts: 'I am zealous for Zion with great zeal; with great fervour I am zealous for her.' "Thus says the LORD: 'I will return to Zion, and dwell in the midst of Jerusalem. Jerusalem shall be called the City of Truth, the Mountain of the LORD of hosts the Holy Mountain.'"
(Zechariah 8:1-3)

Zeal is part of the successful living package, because it causes us to be moved within, it stirs and consumes us and prompts us to take action.

Just as the Apostle Paul exhorted Timothy to stir up the gifts within, we must believe and be ready to stir up our zeal for Kingdom exploits whenever we sense apathy and lukewarmness gripping our hearts.

> *Therefore I remind you to stir up the gift of God which is in you through the laying on of my hands. For God has not given us a spirit of fear, but of power and of love and of a sound mind.*
> *(2 Timothy 1:6-7)*

Stir up zeal. Pray fervently in the Holy Spirit using the gift of tongues, (ask Holy Spirit for this incredible gift if you don't have it). Search the Word of God for Scriptures relating to passion, zeal, fervour, purpose. You will soon find these expressions linked to strength, might and victory!

You are now the representation and reflection of The Lord. His desire remains the same; that through the Ecclesia (The Church that Jesus is building, by the revelation of Who He is - Matthew 16:18-19), others will come to know Him.

DAY THIRTY-THREE

Remain Flexible

Life sometimes throws a curve ball - be flexible and overcome!!

The key to knowing what to do when something in life happens unexpectedly and unannounced is to be flexible and adaptable. This quality of character has to be developed and exercised.

The great athletes can only achieve great feats and release their talents to the best of their ability because of training and exercise.

Jeremiah Chapter eighteen describes the attentive potter as he constructs the prospective slab of clay. It is amazing how the ceramist is able to fashion and form the substance into the most beautiful of objects. Equally incredible is the fact that our lives are like that clay; As the master potter, our heavenly Father promises to mould and shaping us under His careful and skilful Hand. Whilst under the direction of the craftsman, the clay remains soft and pliable on the wheel. So too, does God want us to remain soft, flexible and mouldable.

Determine Your Direction

There are many things that happen in our lives unexpectedly, but as long as we remain in the hands of the Master Potter, we can be moved to adapt and to overcome every time. He loves it when our hearts are pliable - not stiff and hard, unyielding or unteachable.

> *The word which came to Jeremiah from the LORD, saying: "Arise and go down to the potter's house, and there I will cause you to hear My words." Then I went down to the potter's house, and there he was, making something at the wheel. And the vessel that he made of clay was marred in the hand of the potter; so he made it again into another vessel, as it seemed good to the potter to make. Then the word of the LORD came to me, saying: "O house of Israel, can I not do with you as this potter?" says the LORD. "Look, as the clay is in the potter's hand, so are you in My hand, O house of Israel!*
> *(Jeremiah 18:1-6)*

The first piece of clay was marred... This word in Hebrew is **šâḥat** (pronounced *sha-kheth*), and means: *spoiled, ruined, corrupt, perverted, wasted.* I can remember a time in my life when I was rebellious and disobedient to the Lord. I walked into the church service to be met with the news of a visiting speaker that day. I wanted to skip the meeting and leave. One of the leaders of the church noticed my swift turn around as I headed towards the door and he sternly encouraged me to stay, to open my heart to the Lord in worship and to hear what The Lord might say. The preacher spoke on this very Scripture, with particular attention to describing the back of the potter's house where all the unyielding clay was thrown; the clay that was of no use because of its stiff, pliable, obstinate nature. That was certainly a word on time for my soul! I have never forgotten the lesson. Needless to say, it was a great day of repentance and turn around for me.

How about you? Do you need to bend and yield in a fresh way today?

Opening our hearts in worship allows the Holy spirit to wash us and soften us. The Lord is well able to make something new and beautiful out of the marred. He can quite literally make us over!

If you feel that you have become hardened and unyielding, just step under the rain of the Holy Spirit. Let Him drench you and soften you in His love.

Come before the Lord and yield to Him afresh today. Just like me, you won't regret it!

DAY THIRTY-FOUR

Continuing the Journey with Proverbs:

Watch where you are going!

The Book of Proverbs contains thirty-one Chapters and is full of **treasure**. It has been said that if you want to grow in wisdom, knowledge and understanding, you should read, consider and meditate on one chapter of the book of Proverbs each day. You would read through them all twelve times in a year!

I am sure that we all have favourite passages of Scriptures. I committed to memory Proverbs 4:20-23 and Proverbs 6:20-23, many years ago. These Scriptures assure us of the power of the whole counsel of God to lead, keep, watch over, heal and speak to us. It is not enough that we have Scriptures to hand. Most believers in the developed world have access to more Bibles of various translations and resources than we ever need. What counts is what we have committed to memory and allowed to change and shape our lifestyle and behaviour.

Determine Your Direction

Then Jesus said to those Jews who believed Him, "If you abide in My word, you are My disciples indeed. And you shall know the truth, and the truth shall make you free."
(John 8:31-32)

It is the truth that you ***know,*** that actually sets you free and changes you forever!

My son, give attention to my words; incline your ear to my sayings. Do not let them depart from your eyes; keep them in the midst of your heart; for they are life to those who find them, and health to all their flesh. Keep your heart with all diligence, for out of it spring the issues of life. Put away from you a deceitful mouth, and put perverse lips far from you.
(Proverbs 4:20-24)

And here is that same portion of Scripture in The Passion Translation,

Listen carefully, my dear child, to everything that I teach you, and pay attention to all that I have to say. Fill your thoughts with my words until they penetrate deep into your spirit. Then, as you unwrap my words, they will impart true life and radiant health into the very core of your being. So above all, guard the affections of your heart, for they affect all that you are. Pay attention to the

welfare of your innermost being, for from there flows the wellspring of life. Avoid dishonest speech and pretentious words. Be free from using perverse words no matter what!
(Proverbs 4:20-24, TPT)

As you finish up your journey through this devotional, I want to declare over you that your days ahead are going to be filled with purpose, well-being and…life, life, life!

Set your gaze on the path before you. With fixed purpose, looking straight ahead, ignore life's distractions. Watch where you're going! Stick to the path of truth, and the road will be safe and smooth before you. Don't allow yourself to be sidetracked for even a moment or take the detour that leads to darkness.
(Proverbs 4:25-27, TPT)

In the same way you would "set your gaze," so set your mind and the eyes of your heart to "look straight ahead" as you *determine your direction*. My prayer is that as a result of reading and applying the words in this book, you have gained fresh perspective, renewed strength, determination to go for your goals and resilience against the wiles of the devil, together with some tools to help you be an overcomer. (The most important of which is the Word of God and the examples of Jesus Himself.)

Determine Your Direction

Turning to Proverbs chapter 6, though the narrative is discussing godly parents giving good advice to their children, for the sake of the purpose (and hope) of this devotional, I'd like to adapt it by wording it this way:

> *(Let this) wisdom guide you wherever you go and keep you from bringing harm to yourself. (Let this) instruction whisper to you at every sunrise and direct you through a brand-new day. For truth is a bright beam of light shining into every area of your life, instructing and correcting you to discover the ways to godly living.*
> (Taken from Proverbs 6:22-23, TPT, of which verse 22 has been adapted.)

May you be daily launched by Jesus' "bright beam of light" into new realms of glory and revelation, as you continue to ***determine your direction.***

DAY THIRTY-FIVE

Selah Reflection: Understanding Shabbat Rest

We have discussed how there are more labour-saving devices than ever with more technology and information at our disposal (to apparently make life easier), yet we feel more weary and overwhelmed than ever. Rest is given to us in order for us to recover and recuperate. That is why we sleep! We are restored as we rest and we also receive revelation from God when we rest. It is so important that we find ways to cultivate a lifestyle of worship and rest in our weekly rhythm of work or regular chores.

So today, on this final day of this devotional, I'd like to encourage you to:

1. Write out two or three promises that the Lord has fulfilled in your life. These are answered prayers, but also can be occasions where you know the Lord promised something to

you and you had to wait "in faith" for it to be fulfilled.

2. It is during these times, as we rely on and lean into His Word to us, that we grow and develop in faith. Now... Extend your faith for two or three promises that you are waiting for right now. Pray them back to Lord, remind Him of His Word and affirm that you are believing and trusting to see the manifestation.

3. As you take time to worship, yield your heart to the Lord and ask for Holy Spirit to ignite a fresh flame of fiery passion for Jesus - for all that He wants you to share. Take time to offer up fervent prayer for His Bride - the Church - across the world. Until the Bride is completely ready, Jesus will not return. Pray for the fire and passion necessary to cause revival and harvest to be evidenced globally.

4. How have you, or are you currently, experiencing the Potter's Hand? Write in your journal how you are sensing the Lord mould and shape you at this time. Ask Him to make you sensitive and flexible. Allow the Holy Spirit to wash you and soften you in a fresh way.

To conclude your journey, if you would like to, please write a

Selah Reflection: Understanding Shabbat Rest

paragraph detailing two aspects of this devotional journey that you found particularly inspiring, enlightening or encouraging. Share with someone how it has impacted you and anything that has challenged you. What action steps towards establishing your path ahead did you take whilst reading it? I would love to hear from you! Please get in touch with me at: jen@bestlifeever.co.uk

It has been a privilege journeying with you through this *Determine Your Direction* devotional. I pray for you all of God's best.

Footnotes

1. Buckminster Fuller, R. Critical Path. (1981). In 1982 Fuller came up with the "Knowledge Doubling Curve". New York: St Martin's Press
2. Micah 2:13 "The Breaker [the Messiah] will go up before them. They will break through, pass in through the gate and go out through it, and their King will pass on before them, the Lord at their head." (AMPC)
3. 'Thoughts': (Strongs: h4284) מַחֲשָׁבָה mahašaḇa; (concretely) a texture, machine, or (abstractly) intention, plan (whether bad, a plot, or good, advice) thought, device, plan, purpose, invention.
4. Robert Herjavec, The Will to Win: Leading, Competing, Succeeding (2013). "Thinking too much leads to paralysis by analysis. It's important to think things through, but many use thinking as a means of avoiding action." Excerpt taken from Herjavec's book, *The Will To Win*. Published by HarperCollins Canada.
5. Quote by Mary Englebriet.
6. Romans 12:2, "And do not be conformed to this world, but be transformed by the renewing of your mind, that you may prove what *is* that good and acceptable and perfect will of God." (NKJV)
7. Benjamin Franklin Quotes. (n.d.). Retrieved April 13, 2022, from Website:https://www.brainyquote.com/quotes/benjamin_franklin_378118
8. *Dictionary*, Merriam-Webster, Accessed 13 April, 2022
9. Elizabeth Scott. "10 Signs You May Be A Perfectionist". Updated 05, 2022. Elizabeth Scott PHD. Sourced from
10. Ephesians 2:6, "And He raised us up together with Him and made us sit down together [giving us joint seating with Him] in the heavenly sphere [by virtue of our being] in Christ Jesus (the Messiah, the Anointed One)." (AMPC)
11. "Pie in the sky," an American phrase originally coined by US labourer and writer Joe Hill, in 1911. It's meaning is, "a

promise of heaven, while continuing to suffer in this life." Retrieved 13 April, 2022, from h/ses.org.uk/meanings/pie-in-the-sky.html
12. Bickle, M. (2006). "The Seven Longings of the Human Heart." By Mike Bickle with Deborah Hiebert. Published by Forerunner Books, International House of Prayer - Kansas City. https://www.IHOP.org
13. Loretta Young presented producer David Puttnam the Oscar for "Best Picture" for *Chariots Of Fire*, at the 54th Academy Awards, Hosted by Johnny Carson. The film was written by Vangelis.
14. Eric Henry Liddell, whom Oscar winning film Chariots of Fire is filmed after. Cited from Wikipedia, https://www.en.m.wikipedia.org/wiki/Eric_Liddell
15. See Exodus 16:23, 'He told them, "This is what the LORD commanded: Tomorrow will be a day of complete rest, a holy Sabbath day set apart for the LORD. So, bake or boil as much as you want today, and set aside what is left for tomorrow."' (NLT) For the *Ten Commandments*, see Exodus 20:2-17 and Deuteronomy 5:6-21.
16. The phrase "every touch leaves a trace," was coined by Dr. Edmund Locard (1877-1966), a pioneer in forensic science. To learn more, visit https://theknowledgeburrow.com
17. The "Parable of the Sower" can be found in Matthew 13:1-23, Mark 4:1-20 and Luke 8:4-15.
18. Harry S. Truman was the thirty-third President of the United States (1945 - 1953), succeeding Franklin D Roosevelt. Truman was an author and known for coming up with some impactful quotes, of which "Not all readers are leaders, but all leaders are readers" is one.
19. Comer, John Mark. (2019). "The Ruthless Elimination of Hurry: How to stay emotionally healthy and spiritually alive in the chaos of the modern world." Published by John Murray Press, October 2019.
20. The second book of Samuel's reference (2 Samuel 22:33) opens slightly differently to Psalm 18:32. While Psalm 18 is written, "It is God who arms me with strength, and makes my way perfect," second Samuel reads, "God is my strength and power,

and He makes my way perfect..."
21. This took place in the time of King Cyrus of Babylon around 538 BC, when he decreed, the Jews were allowed to return to the land of Israel. Many remained however, because they had settled. But those who left went on to help rebuild the temple to the God of Israel, Yahweh.
22. Victor Borge. (1909-2000). "Laughter is the shortest distance between two people." Quote taken from *The Walking Book (1979)*. Source of information retrieved from https://libquotes.com/victor-borge/quote/ibt6c0c
23. biblehub.com. (2004-2021). Barnes' commentary on Ecclesiastes 7:6. Sourced at https://biblehub.com/commentaries/ecclesiastes/7-6.htm
24. The story of Joseph Grimaldi. Visit https://en.m.wikipedia.org/wiki/Joseph_Grimaldi
25. It is generally not known who wrote this Psalm. However according to the *Matthew Henry Commentary on the Whole Bible*, it is the "opinion of some of the Jewish writers...that this Psalm was penned and sung by Adam in innocence, on the first Sabbath." However, Henry draws out inconsistencies with the subject matter of the Psalm in relation to sin not having yet entered the world on the first ever Sabbath. He therefore denotes that it is more likely to be David who wrote this Psalm. For source information, https://www.blueletterbible.org/comm/mhc/Psa/Psa_092.cfm
26. Leo Buscaglia (full name Felice Leonardo Buscaglia), lived from March 31, 1924 - June 12th, 1998. An American author, motivational speaker and professor in the Dept. of Special Education at the University of Southern California, Leo was also known as "Dr. Love". Sourced from https://en.m.wikipedia/wiki/Leo_Buscaglia
27. Definition of strategy. Retrieved from https://www.oxfordreference.com
28. Walt Disney Quotes. BrainyMedia Inc, 2022. 24 April 2022. https://www.brainyquote.com/quotes/walt_disney_163027
29. John Eckhardt. (2011). "Prayers That Activate Blessings". Published by Charisma House

Stay Connected

I recently read this:

> If you want to move fast, travel alone.
> If you want to travel a long way, find your tribe.

I am inviting you to join our community **BestLifeEver** facebook group, where you will find encouragement together with others pursuing the path onwards and upwards to greater exploits and adventures. It is a place to connect, develop and grow. See you there!

Please send a testimonial of how this **Determine Your Direction** Devotional Journey has impacted you to jen@bestlifeever.co.uk

Visit my web site: jenwatson.co.uk where you will find free PDF notes, information about upcoming events, webinar details and offers.

Public Facebook Group: **Best Life Ever**

You may also further connect (subscribe, follow and like) …

(YouTube) Jen Watson https://bit.ly/SubscribetomyYTchannel

(Instagram) @jenn.watson10

(Facebook) @jenn.watson10

(Twitter) @jennwatson1010

Blessings,

Jenny

Moving Forward, Reaching Goals,

Doing Exploits...

Everyone experiences seasons of growth and development, everything is going well and we are flourishing, as well as seasons of inactivity and rest. But how do you jump start from a place of procrastination, failure or simply not knowing the next step. "Where next" and "how to" are familiar questions we ask ourselves.

This devotional journey will enable you to set your internal compass towards true north, the upward call, at a daily steady pace. Interspersed with *Selah Shabbat pauses* to give time for reflection and refocus.

Join the journey to **Determine Your Direction.** The place ahead is bright, broad, and bountiful for those walking hand in hand with Jesus.

Jenny Watson is an inspiring communicator and leader. Married to Stephen for 34 years, together they established *Kingdom Advance Network,* a Prophetic Apostolic Centre in the Midlands, UK. Jenny is passionate about strengthening the Body of Christ and equipping in Spiritual Warfare, Prophecy and Hearing God's Voice, God's Appointed Times and Worship Lifestyle. Jenny is a gifted worship leader and mentor to many.

Printed in Great Britain
by Amazon